THE GREAT QUESTIONS OF PHILOSOPHY AND PHYSICS

STEVEN GIMBEL, PhD

4840 Westfields Boulevard | Suite 500 | Chantilly, Virginia | 20151-2299
[PHONE] 1.800.832.2412 | [FAX] 703.378.3819 | [WEB] www.thegreatcourses.com

LEADERSHIP

PAUL SUIJK	President & CEO
BRUCE G. WILLIS	Chief Financial Officer
JOSEPH PECKL	SVP, Marketing
JASON SMIGEL	VP, Product Development
CALE PRITCHETT	VP, Marketing
MARK LEONARD	VP, Technology Services
DEBRA STORMS	VP, General Counsel
KEVIN MANZEL	Sr. Director, Content Development
ANDREAS BURGSTALLER	Sr. Director, Brand Marketing & Innovation
KEVIN BARNHILL	Director of Creative
GAIL GLEESON	Director, Business Operations & Planning

PRODUCTION TEAM

DEREK KNIGHT	Producer
SUSAN DYER	Content Developer
MASHA STOYANOVA	Associate Producer
DANIEL RODRIGUEZ	Graphic Artist
OWEN YOUNG	Managing Editor
ANDREW VOLPE	Editor
CHARLES GRAHAM	Assistant Editor
GORDON HALL IV	Audio Engineer
GEORGE BOLDEN KELLY TAGLIAFERRI	Camera Operators
VALERIE WELCH	Production Assistant
JIM M. ALLEN	Director

PUBLICATIONS TEAM

FARHAD HOSSAIN	Publications Manager
MARTIN STEGER	Copyeditor
JUSTIN RINONOS	Graphic Designer
JESSICA MULLINS	Proofreader
ERIKA ROBERTS	Publications Assistant
VICTORIA CHIN JEN ROSENBERG	Fact-Checkers
WILLIAM DOMANSKI	Transcript Editor & Fact-Checker

Copyright © The Teaching Company, 2020

Printed in the United States of America

This book is in copyright. All rights reserved. Without limiting the rights under copyright reserved above, no part of this publication may be reproduced, stored in or introduced into a retrieval system, or transmitted, in any form, or by any means (electronic, mechanical, photocopying, recording, or otherwise), without the prior written permission of The Teaching Company.

Steven Gimbel is a Professor of Philosophy at Gettysburg College, where he also served as chair of the Philosophy Department. He received his PhD in Philosophy from Johns Hopkins University. At Gettysburg College, he has received the Luther W. and Bernice L. Thompson Distinguished Teaching Award and was named to the Edwin T. and Cynthia Shearer Johnson Chair for Distinguished Teaching in the Humanities.

Professor Gimbel's research focuses on the philosophy of science, especially the philosophy of physics. He has also published papers on the philosophy of language, ethics, and the philosophy of humor. Professor Gimbel is the author of more than 40 journal articles and book chapters as well as seven books, including *Isn't That Clever: A Philosophical Account of Humor and Comedy*; *Defending Einstein: Hans Reichenbach's Early Writings on Space, Time, and Motion*; *Exploring the Scientific Method: Cases and Questions*; *Einstein's Jewish Science: Physics at the Intersection of Politics and Religion*; *Einstein: His Space and Times*; and *The Grateful Dead and Philosophy: Getting High Minded about Love and Haight*.

Professor Gimbel's other Great Courses include *Redefining Reality: The Intellectual Implications of Modern Science*; *An Introduction to Formal Logic*; and *Take My Course, Please! The Philosophy of Humor*.

TABLE OF CONTENTS

Introduction

Professor Biography i
Course Scope 1

Guides

1. Does Physics Make Philosophy Superfluous? 3
2. Why Mathematics Works So Well with Physics 12
3. Can Physics Explain Reality? 22
4. The Reality of Einstein's Space 31
5. The Nature of Einstein's Time 41
6. The Beginning of Time 50
7. Are Atoms Real? 59
8. Quantum States: Neither True nor False? 70
9. Waves, Particles, and Quantum Entanglement 83
10. Wanted Dead and Alive: Schrödinger's Cat 92
11. The Dream of Grand Unification 99
12. The Physics of God 110

Supplementary Material

Quiz Answer Key 118
Bibliography 120

Great Questions of Philosophy

This lecture series examines the philosophical questions raised by our best scientific theories about matter, energy, space, and time. We will set out contentious philosophical problems that arise out of our attempt to mathematically explain the nature of the universe and look at the different, often-contrasting views that seek to solve them. All of the philosophers who wrestle with these problems have extensive backgrounds in physics, and all of the physicists who weigh in are cognizant of the deeply philosophical ramifications of their work.

The course's 12 lectures are divided into four groups. The first three lectures set the table for the series by looking at high-level questions about the relationship between the two fields of study. The first lecture defines what is meant by the terms *philosophy* and *physics* and examines the methods and subfields of the two disciplines. The second lecture examines the relationship between physics and mathematics, and the third lecture looks at the nature of scientific explanations in physics.

The second group, comprised of the fourth through sixth lectures, examines questions about the nature of space and time. For instance, is space real? If we take all of the matter and energy out of the universe, is there anything left? Does time have a beginning? We will look at the concepts used in classical physics—that is, concepts involved in the theory of Isaac Newton and how those concepts changed with Albert Einstein's theories of relativity. Einstein's theories make better predictions than Newton, but do they also solve the conceptual problems concerning the basic notions of mass, energy, space, time, and motion? Surely, the picture they paint of reality is more complex, but are the basic concepts of space and time better understood?

In the third group, made up of the seventh through tenth lectures, we turn from space and time to matter. We examine the evidence that gave rise to atomic theory. How can science, which is based on observation, tell us that reality is comprised of something too small to be seen? Attempts to understand how these atoms behave gave rise in the first half of the 20th century to quantum mechanics, perhaps the strangest scientific theory to ever be created. We will look at the philosophical issues raised by the Heisenberg uncertainty principle and the probabilities that plague the theory in ways that seemingly cannot be eliminated.

In the final two lectures, we ask the biggest of the big questions. Is it possible to have a single unified theory of everything? Einstein's theory of relativity has never been wrong. Neither has quantum mechanics. However, it turns out that they cannot both be true. Is there a possible way to unify them? What if our attempts at unification imply the universe looks nothing like what we see? Do these theories that describe the origin of the universe point to the existence of God? Do they point to the existence of multiple universes? These are the provocative questions tackled by this course.

DOES PHYSICS MAKE PHILOSOPHY SUPERFLUOUS?

LECTURE 1

The philosophical problems examined in this course arise from the study of physics, though physicists and philosophers have very different jobs. This lecture sets out what philosophy is, what physics is, and examines how philosophy of physics came to be. It also begins to look at some of the philosophical questions that arise out of physics.

Defining Physics

Physics is the scientific study of the nonliving part of the natural world, or at least the study that does not worry about the nature of life. Physics begins with the presupposition that we live in an ordered universe. The objects and events that are part of the universe follow certain rules, and those rules are accessible to the human mind. We call them laws of nature. Physics is the search for these laws of nature.

The branches of physics correspond to seemingly distinct sorts of phenomena which we observe. Traditionally, there are eight branches of physics:

1. Mechanics—the study of objects in motion.

2. Gravitation—the study of the attraction between objects.

3. Thermodynamics—the study of heat.

4. Electricity—the study of electrical charge.

5. Magnetism—the study of magnetic forces.

6. Optics—the study of light.

7. Material science—the science of matter.

8. Astronomy/cosmology—the study of things we see in the sky, especially their origin.

Branches and Subfields

The history of physics has caused a number of these eight branches to join together while at the same time further branching into subfields. In the 17th century, Isaac Newton gave us the most important theory in the history of humanity. It combined mechanics and gravitation.

In the 19th century, James Clerk Maxwell framed the kinetic theory of heat, arguing that matter was comprised of molecules and that heat was the motion of these molecules. This meant that heat was really just motion, and so thermodynamic properties like temperature and pressure could be explained mechanically. In turn, thermodynamics reduced to mechanics. That reduction led a need for statistical laws to describe the motion of great collections of molecules, which is called statistical mechanics.

Maxwell also collected laws about electricity and magnetism and showed that these two seemingly distinct physical phenomena were just flip sides of the same coin. He thus united them into a single theory of electromagnetism. He went on to show that light was an electromagnetic wave, thereby bringing optics under the umbrella of electromagnetism. This meant that mechanics, gravitation, and thermodynamics were one unified branch and electricity, magnetism, and optics were another.

Albert Einstein, with his work in the first half of the 20th century, then brought these two together through his work on relativity. Matter remained its own branch. Through the 20th century, physicists examined the nature of matter. Figures like J. J. Thomson, Ernest Rutherford, and Niels Bohr developed atomic theory, according to which molecules were atoms that were made up of charged, massive particles like electrons, protons, and neutrons.

Bohr led the way to quantum theory, which in turn led the Standard Model, our best current account of the universe and its behavior at the smallest scale. Different states of matter behave differently. Solids are unlike liquids, and adding enough energy creates plasma. As a result, there are different subfields, including solid state physics, high energy physics, plasma physics, and nuclear physics. The hope is to unify all of this with the rest of physics, but this has proven a challenge. Cosmology has come to be one place where the results of all of the other branches are utilized.

Defining Philosophy

Philosophy does not study observable phenomena. If there is a question that is answered by observation, that is a scientific question, not a philosophical one. Philosophy is concerned with a priori questions—that is, questions that are prior to experience. Philosophers ask questions whose answers do not require investigation into the behavior of the world. There are four branches to philosophy:

1. Logic—the study of rational argumentation.

2. Epistemology—the study of knowledge.

3. Metaphysics—the study of reality.

4. Axiology—the study of value judgments. Its two subfields are ethics (the study of value judgments regarding right and wrong for free human actions) and aesthetics (the study of value judgments concerning beauty).

Physics gives rise to questions in all four branches. The vast majority of the questions, though, fall under metaphysics and epistemology.

> At one time, science was a part of philosophy. Along with virtually every other field of study, physics begins with the philosophy of Aristotle, perhaps the most brilliant human ever to walk the planet.

SCIENCE AS A PART OF PHILOSOPHY

Axiology: Aesthetics

This course looks mainly at logic, epistemology, and metaphysics. However, this lecture closes with a look at axiology, starting with aesthetics. Notable scientific figures—including Albert Einstein, Nobel Laureate Richard Feynman, and Einstein-influencer Henri Poincaré—have made versions of the following argument:

1. Nature is beautiful.

2. This beauty consists, at least in part, but essentially, in its coherence and simplicity.

3. Science is the process by which we craft linguistic/mathematical representations of nature.

4. Representations mirror the internal structure of that which they represent.

5. Therefore, because the beauty of nature is in its structure, science—if it is to be effective—will be beautiful.

A philosopher might argue with this. For example, take Peter Achinstein, professor of philosophy and author of the book *Speculation in and about Science*. He argues that the second premise in the argument the scientists made is false. Achinstein agrees that beauty, coherence, and simplicity are all virtues of a scientific theory. He calls them pragmatic virtues because they are useful and helpful aspects that we do desire in our scientific theories.

We want our theories to be beautiful because the coherence and simplicity make scientific theories easier to use. They allow for better, more understandable explanations. They allow us to picture the underlying causes more easily and in a way that can lead to further advances.

However, the reason there will need to be further advances, Achinstein argues, is because that is not how nature really is. He argues that when we look at case after case, we see approximations, simplifications, and speculations. The question is not whether nature really is that way, but whether this simplified representation works.

The question then becomes what it works for. The great theories will work for a lot, but not for everything. There will be more intricate questions about nature in which the simplified representation will fail to do what we need it to do. The result is that the theory becomes more complicated because nature is more complicated.

Axiology: Ethics

The other aspect of axiology is ethics. Physics is an activity done by humans. Any time people engage in a project, there will always be moral questions. The moral questions surrounding physics often have to do with its abstractness. Physics studies aspects of the world that are so fundamental that they are often quite removed from everyday life. However, because of how fundamental the questions are, the tools that are needed to answer questions are so intricate and often large that they are incredibly expensive.

We live in a world in which there is dire poverty. We have fellow humans who do not have their basic needs met. Is the abstract knowledge that physics seeks so valuable that we should take funds that could go to helping the needy to find it?

One argument says yes. To be human is to wonder about the world. To stop funding science is to rob us of an essential aspect of our own humanity.

Another argument in favor of funding physics is to argue that we should be able to fund both. The pitting of science and the well-being of those in need is a false choice. Both of these ought to be priorities, and both ought to be funded by cutting back on the much larger spending for other less virtuous activities.

A third argument is utilitarian. Science has positive technological benefits, so we should fund it for those unforeseen advances that will be helpful.

This leads to a completely different question: If we justify science through the technological advances, does that not also mean that we should hold science and scientists morally culpable when the advances cause harm? Are physicists morally responsible for the uses to which their physics is put by our society? Do physicists have special moral obligations to advise and advocate on science policy?

Out of fear that the Nazis could do it first, Einstein wrote a letter to President Roosevelt urging the United States to develop nuclear weapons. After the dropping of those weapons on Japanese cities, Einstein was reported as having said, "I could burn my fingers that I wrote that letter."

Is Einstein, at least in part, responsible for the deaths caused by the dropping of the atomic bombs? He spent his later years advocating against the further development of atom weapons.

Suggested Reading

Ayer, *Language, Truth, and Logic*.
Blackburn, *Think*.
Toulmin and Goodfield, *The Fabric of the Heavens*.

QUIZ QUESTIONS

1. What is mechanics the physical study of?

    A. Heat.
    B. Light.
    C. Motion.
    D. Matter.

2. What is the difference between astronomy and cosmology?

3. What does the Latin term *a priori* mean?

4. Which is the study of knowledge: epistemology or axiology?

5. What did the logical positivists mean by a criterion of cognitive significance?

ANSWERS KEY CAN BE FOUND ON PAGE 118

WHY MATHEMATICS WORKS SO WELL WITH PHYSICS

LECTURE 2

We associate science, especially physics, with mathematics. So close is the relation that we now speak in terms of the acronym STEM, meaning science, technology, engineering, and mathematics. There are wonderful pop science books that explain the most famous equations in the history of physics. Physics and mathematics are thought of as inextricably intertwined. This was not always the case. It was only in the 1700s that mathematical physics began to emerge. Before that, physics read like philosophy—because it was.

The Early Days

There were some limited applications of mathematics to nature early on, largely in astronomy. Aside from that, there really was no mathematics anywhere in physics. The person who started to change that was Galileo. He developed an equation for bodies in gravitational freefall. It was an incredible advance, but it was limited by a lack of powerful mathematics.

That changed with René Descartes's analytic geometry. Prior to Descartes, it was thought that there were two distinct branches of mathematics. One was number theory, made up of algebra, arithmetic, and the like. This dealt with quantitative matters. The other was geometry, which dealt with more qualitative shapes in space.

Descartes figured out that through graphing, it is possible to develop a translation dictionary between geometry and algebra. It was now possible to talk about the equations of lines, parabolas, and circles. This opened the door to mathematically modeling more complex matters like trajectories.

This still wasn't powerful enough. That need was filled in the next generation by Isaac Newton with his theory of fluxions, or calculus, as it is now known. With calculus, physics could become fully mathematized. This successful project caught the attention of Eugene Wigner.

Wigner's Impact

Born in Budapest in 1902, Wigner studied both mathematics and physics. He was one of the individuals who brought cutting-edge mathematical theory into physics when quantum mechanics was raising difficult questions about the nature of the atom. He was the assistant to David Hilbert, the most important figure in turn-of-the-century mathematics.

In 1960, Wigner wrote a famous piece entitled "The Unreasonable Effectiveness of Mathematics in the Natural Sciences." He raises this issue: Math works incredibly well in allowing us to come up with unexpected predictions. It seems miraculous. What is it about mathematics that allows this to happen?

Max Tegmark, a physics professor, has proposed one answer: The world is a mathematical system. Tegmark considers two hypotheses. The first is what he calls the external reality hypothesis, or the ERH. This asserts that there is a universe, humans are in it, and humans have experiences of it. However, we have experiences of things independent of us and our experiences. If a person looks and sees a chair, it is because there is a chair for the person to see.

Theories are comprised of two parts. One part is the strictly mathematical content that seeks to describe the world as it is. But mixed in with this is what Tegmark terms *baggage*—that is, aspects that we use to connect this formalism to our experiences. The baggage in our theories is the parts that refer to human experience, and the goal of real science is to ultimately produce a theory that is stripped of all of this baggage.

To do so would be to validate the second hypothesis, the mathematical universe hypothesis, or MUH, which asserts, "Our external reality is a mathematical structure." There are three parts to this statement. The external reality is what comes from the external reality hypothesis. A mathematical structure is a baggage-free system of abstract concepts in a specified system of relations. The third part of the hypothesis is the single word *is*.

There are different meanings of *is*. In this case, it means the is of identity, but the notion of identity is a specific type: mathematical identity. Two mathematical structures are identical if one can map them onto and into each other—that is, if there is an isomorphism. Because mathematics is a language of bare relationships, if two systems are different ways of describing the same relationships, then they are different ways of saying the same thing. Thus, the two structures are to be deemed the same structure.

There are two different ways people do science. One is starting with baggage—that is, we look around the world, see what is happening, and come up with theories to explain it. However, as we develop better and better theories, we can start to strip out the baggage, leaving more and more pure, abstract, mathematical theories.

Tegmark argues that if science is successful, then science will have created a mathematical system that is isomorphic to the world it describes. This means that the world is the mathematical system.

Willard van Orman Quine and Hilary Putnam

A similar but distinct explanation came from two of the biggest names in 20th-century philosophy, Willard van Orman Quine and Hilary Putnam. The two were colleagues and dear friends in the philosophy department at Harvard for decades.

Both rose to prominence after the fall of logical positivism, which was the start of modern philosophy of physics. Logical positivism is based on four pillars:

1. A criterion of cognitive significance that allows us to determine which sentences say something meaningful and which are simply intelligent-sounding nonsense.

2. The analytic/synthetic distinction, which divides the meaningful propositions into those that are necessary truths from those that are contingent truths.

3. A theory of analytic truths—that is, a philosophy of math.

4. A theory of contingent truths—that is, a philosophy of science.

Quine and Putnam were among those who brought the fall of logical positivism about. One of Quine's most famous works is a paper entitled "Two Dogmas of Empiricism." By *empiricism*, he means logical positivism.

The first of the two dogmas is reductionism: that we can reduce all true propositions to combinations of logic and sense perception. This was the heart of the first pillar of logical positivism. The second dogma is the analytic/synthetic distinction. This receives the most attention in the article and is the dogma Quine undermines.

The analytic/synthetic distinction separates meaningful sentences into two different classes. There are necessary truths: sentences whose negations are contradictions. There are contingent truths: sentences whose negations are still possible. Quine shows that there is no clean way to draw this line.

We could consider the mathematics to be analytic—that is, to be necessary. That leaves our scientific beliefs underdetermined: They would be synthetic. However, he argues, we could declare absolute belief in certain possible laws of physics. We could declare them necessarily true. Doing so is possible, but then the sentences of mathematics become contingent.

The web as a whole is confirmed by our experience, Quine argues, but then it is up to us which strands of the web we declare to be analytic and which to be synthetic. In other words, it is up to us which parts are true by definition and which parts are contingent facts of the world. Based on this picture, the two figures developed what has come to be known as the Quine-Putnam indispensability thesis, which concludes that numbers exist as objects in the world just as much as atoms.

The Existence of Numbers

The logical positivists had an aversion to metaphysics. They wanted a universe as scarcely populated as possible. If one did not have observable evidence for the existence of something, it was not a thing. Mathematical concepts surely were not things. Math, they held, was the language of physics. It provided the grammatical structure and nothing more.

Take the equation $E = mc^2$. In it, there are three symbols. The m and the c are measurable quantities and as such represent things. The E is not directly measurable, but it is defined in terms of measurables and so is a theoretical term. It does not refer to something in the world but is reduceable to the observables that do exist.

There are also the equal sign and the exponent 2. These are non-referring terms. They don't point out anything in reality; they merely provide the linguistic structure needed to say things about things in reality. However, this picture hinges on a working and absolute analytic/synthetic distinction. Once that is gone, we have to ask anew: What do the equations of physics tell us exists in the universe?

Quine and Putnam argue that whatever is indispensable in our best physical theories ought to be held to exist. In this view, our mathematical notions need to be considered to be real things in the universe.

An Objection

The most notable objection to Quine and Putnam on this matter is that of Hartry Field. Field earned his PhD at Harvard writing under Hilary Putnam. For this lecture's purposes, his most important work is his first book: *Science without Numbers*.

Field wants to be able to reconstruct physics in a way that does not make use of numbers. He is not saying that numbers are not useful in physics. They are. However, the Quine-Putnam argument says more than that they are useful; it hinges on the claim that mathematical machinery is indispensable.

Field starts his move to eliminate mathematics with the work of a mathematician, David Hilbert. He came from Königsberg, an area that used to be part of Germany but is now part of Russia.

Hilbert thought about Euclidean geometry. Euclid's work is a masterpiece of rigor, but mathematicians had long known that there were a few flaws in that diamond. Euclid had made use of a few assumptions that he had not made explicit and a couple of logical leaps. Hilbert would fix it.

Hilbert wrote *Foundations of Geometry*, in which he re-axiomatized Euclid's geometry. He did not start where Euclid did.

Euclid began with definitions. He wanted geometric terms like *point*, *line*, and *plane* to have clear geometric meanings. Hilbert, on the other hand, defines nothing. For him, mathematics is not about meaning but about logical relations. There are no points, lines, or planes in his geometric universe, just a set of rigorously set out logical relations among concepts. As Hilbert famously put it, "Instead of point, line, and plane, one must always be able to say table, chair, and beer mug."

One can see why this approach would be attractive to Field. Hilbert succeeded in reducing geometry to its logical core, not making essential use of any of the notions that represent things. The goal for Field is to create a purely logical set of relations that give us Newtonian mechanics and gravitation.

Field uses logical tools that he very carefully selects so as to be able to do what Hilbert did. The details very technical, and there are a few places where the details are a bit schematic, as Field himself admits. However, the point is that he does an incredible job constructing something that does seem to do what one would need to do to sketch the outline of what Newton's theory does. He does it all without numerical equations.

Some buy into Field's project. Others do not. If it is successful, it will say numbers are not indispensable. If that is correct, it does not answer Wigner's question but rather reopens it.

Suggested Reading

Reid, *Hilbert*.

Tegmark, "The Mathematical Universe."

Wigner, "The Unreasonable Effectiveness of Mathematics in the Natural Sciences"

QUIZ QUESTIONS

1. What does Galileo's equation govern?

    A.   Objects in gravitational freefall.
    B.   The temperature of an object.
    C.   The mass of an object in orbit.
    D.   The period of Earth's motion around the Sun.

2. True or false: Eugene Wigner thinks that physics should use concepts like negative numbers and imaginary numbers that do not correspond to observable concepts.

3. Why does Max Tegmark contend that science begins like a "frog in a bog?" Why does it change?

4. True or false: Willard van Orman Quine and Hilary Putnam consider numbers to be real things, not just useful fictional concepts constructed by humans.

5. What great 19th- and 20th-century mathematician re-axiomatized Euclid's geometry in his book *Foundations of Geometry*?

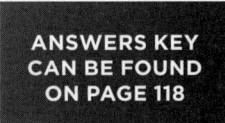

ANSWERS KEY CAN BE FOUND ON PAGE 118

CAN PHYSICS EXPLAIN REALITY?

LECTURE 3

The purpose of physics is seemingly to explain the behavior of the universe and the things in it: What is the universe, and what exactly is in it? Those are empirical questions for the scientist. However, determining the meaning of an explanation is a task for the philosopher. This lecture asks the following questions: What is an explanation? What makes some explanations scientific? Does physics actually explain anything?

Aristotle

The first philosopher to wrestle with such questions was Aristotle. He explicitly says that the purpose of science is to set out the causes of natural phenomena. Additionally, he says that the word *cause* has four completely different meanings. If one were to come across a statue and ask, "What is the cause of this work of art?" one could be asking any one of four questions and thereby could be rightly given any one of four answers:

> Why is there a statue here instead of nothing? The answer is the marble of which the statue is composed. The matter is one cause for the thing it comprises. This is the material cause.

> Why is it this statue? The answer is the shape. The form of the thing causes it to be what it is. This is the formal cause.

> The third notion of cause that Aristotle employs is that of efficient cause. It is the process by which something was brought about. For the statue, the efficient cause was the chiseling of the artist.

> The fourth cause for Aristotle is known as the final cause. The final cause is the purpose a thing serves. It's that for the sake of which a thing was brought about. For instance, the statue's final cause might be to worship a god depicted.

Final cause makes sense whenever we are dealing with individuals to whom we attribute free will. To explain human behavior, we need to account for volition: What is the end that this act was intended to serve?

For Aristotle, that question also makes sense in physics. Like most Greek thinkers of his period, Aristotle bought into the view called teleology. This is the view that all things possess a purpose. Everything happens to serve a plan or is a cog in a larger machine that itself has a purpose.

Aristotle held that physics requires teleological explanations. Why does a rock fall? It has a desire to return to its natural place. When a person lets go of a rock, it will—for internal reasons—seek its natural place. It has a goal. It wants to be at rest in its natural place.

New Theories

In the 17th century, René Descartes proposed the mechanical philosophy as a foundation to physics. All material happenings were to be explained in terms of material interactions. Only pushes and pulls of thing against thing can be posited to explain motion.

One problem was the motion of the planets around the sun. What purely mechanical explanation could there be for that? To fix this problem, Descartes made space into matter, in turn making it able to push other matter.

Descartes's physical theory of gravitation—and his mechanical philosophy—were replaced a few decades later by Isaac Newton with a new theory of gravitation. That theory posited a gravitational force between any two massive objects. The force operates along the line connecting the centers of mass of the two. It is proportional to the product of the masses and inversely proportional to the square of the distance. Gravity is a force across space generated by the mass of the objects, and there is an incredibly accurate formula to describe behavior as a result of it.

Newton himself thought that his theory did not explain anything. There was a cause, but it was not a physical cause. Explanation, Newton thought, requires an appeal to metaphysics. Physics itself is not enough to generate an explanation.

Bertrand Russell

Bertrand Russell, at the beginning of the 20th century, thought that Newton was partially right. In a paper he wrote in 1912 entitled "On the Notion of Cause," Russell tries to remedy the situation. He argues that there are no causes in nature. Newton was right to separate cause from physics but wrong to incorporate it into theology. The famously atheistic Russell wants to finish the job by removing all teleological notions from science.

Russell tries repeatedly to take the commonsense understanding of cause and work it out rigorously. Problems surface each time. The whole notion, he argues, seems to be desired because we cannot give up our desire to achieve the sort of explanation that we can get from a person who can explain her intention in setting things up a certain way. We want nature to have an intelligently expressed will. The search for causes in nature is just an attempt to put God in the working of the world. It is a theological aftereffect, a remnant left in science.

He argues the entire concept of cause in physics is antiquated and obsolete. In his view, we have to jettison the notion of cause and effect. What remains are formulas.

After Russell

An attempt to reconstruct the notion of physical explanation came after Russell. This involved the casting of explanation in terms purely of the relations of observed phenomena and laws. The key figure in this was the German philosopher Carl Gustav Hempel, who had to flee Germany in the buildup to the Third Reich in part because he was Jewish.

Hempel had two models of explanation in physics: the deductive-nomological (or D-N) model and the inductive-statistical (or I-S) model. According to the deductive-nomological account of scientific explanation for physics, an observed phenomenon is explained if we can deductively derive its occurrence from a law of nature. For a law to explain an observed phenomenon, the law must be true. A false law does not explain anything. A legitimate physical explanation occurs when one can show that something someone saw is a direct logical consequence of a true law of nature. The law of nature explains what the person saw. That is how physics explains the world.

However, the I-S model is needed to complement the D-N model. In physics, there are certain cases in which the laws of nature are statistical. Quantum mechanics and statistical mechanics are just two examples of fields in physics with statistical laws. In these cases, explanation will have to be slightly different. With statistical laws, the logical derivation uses a different logic: induction.

Deductive logic gives absolutely certain conclusions because the content of the conclusion is contained within the content of the premises. With induction, the content of the conclusion outruns the content of the premises. The conclusion is a generalization larger than the information in the premise set. Therefore, we cannot have absolute certainty about the truth of the conclusion, but we can have high probability of truth.

It is possible to create an inductive version of the D-N model of explanation. Imagine a phenomenon called P. If there is a true statistical law about P-type events, and one can show through an inductive argument that we should expect P to probably happen as a result of this law, then the law explains the event.

Explaining Laws and Objections

If laws explain phenomena, what explains the laws? In some cases, the answer is being able to derive them from more general laws. Kepler's laws of planetary motion, for example, can be deductively derived from Newton's laws of motion and gravitation.

There have been objections to Hempel's accounts of how explanations in physics work. One standard objection is that Hempel allows too much to count as legitimate scientific explanation.

Another objection goes in the other direction. This objection is raised by Nancy Cartwright from her book *How the Laws of Physics Lie*.

We want science to do two things: give us truth about how the universe works and explain things. Cartwright points out that in Hempel's view, it is the truth of the laws that accounts for their explanatory power. Cartwright contends that Hempel is wrong that explanatory power comes from truth. Indeed, he is wrong that they are compatible.

The truth, Cartwright argues, does not explain much. Truth and explanation are incompatible. When we search for truth, we lose the ability to explain, and good explanations are not true explanations. Physics is at its explanatory best when it stops worrying so much about truth.

The argument begins by pointing out that much of what we treat as laws of nature aren't quite that. The example she gives is Snell's law. It is the reason why a stick half in water looks bent. In a standard optics textbook, Cartwright finds the law initially presented on page 21. The law says that the angle of a light ray moving from one substance to the other will depend on the ratio of the indices of refraction of the two materials. The thicker a material, the more the light will bend in coming through it. Water is thicker than air, so the bending is greater in water. This is why the stick appears to bend when it is halfway submerged.

Snell's law appears again 500 pages later, but now it is the "refined version" of the law. The refinement limits the applicability of the law to optically isotropic media—that is, light moves through it in the same way regardless of direction. In the real world, most media are not really optically isotropic. They are more or less isotropic in a way that makes Snell's law a good working approximation of the actual, much more complex reality.

The law is not a law. It is not literally true of almost anything. And this is the case in general, Cartwright points out. There are no simple relations describable by straightforward equations in reality. The world is messier than our clean theories lead us to believe.

Science has conflicting goals in seeking truth and seeking to explain. We have to neglect one when we work for the other. Science, when it seeks to explain, is like theater, Professor Cartwright argues. Good theater can express human truth, but it does it by creating characters who embody human qualities.

The characters are not deep and round, do not have complete lives, and lack the full complexity of true humanity. However, they represent it well enough to be able to say something deep. We leave good theater thinking we have learned something about the human condition. In the same way, Cartwright argues, we leave good physical explanations thinking we have learned something about the universe, even though we learned it from a simplification.

Suggested Reading

Cartwright, *How the Laws of Physics Lie*.
Hempel, "Studies in the Logic of Confirmation."
Russell, "On the Notion of Cause"

QUIZ QUESTIONS

1. If one were to ask for the material cause of a diamond, the answer should be:

   A. The pyramidal arrangement of the carbon atoms in the diamond.
   B. The carbon atoms making up the diamond.
   C. The pressure that turned the coal into a diamond.
   D. The hardness of the diamond.

2. True or false: Descartes thinks that space is not a material object.

3. Bertrand Russell wanted to remove what concept from the discussion of science?

4. What does the word *nomological* mean?

ANSWERS KEY CAN BE FOUND ON PAGE 118

THE REALITY OF EINSTEIN'S SPACE

LECTURE 4

Some people believe that space itself is a substance. They are known as substantivalists. Relationists, meanwhile, contend that space is not an independent thing. Instead, space is simply the set of relations among things. The argument over these beliefs famously pitted two of the most intelligent humans to ever walk the earth against each other: Isaac Newton and Gottfried Leibniz.

Newton's and Leibniz's Positions

Newton had made his case in his masterwork, *The Mathematical Principles of Natural Philosophy*. Newton argues that space is absolute—that is, a real thing that sits beneath the universe. In addition to space, he argues that time is also absolute.

If space is real, then there is an absolute location for everything in the universe. To move from one absolute location to another over a period of real time means that a thing has absolute motion. Location, velocity, and acceleration are therefore real aspects of the real world.

Leibniz disagreed, putting forth an argument based on a metaphysical axiom he calls the principle of the identity of indiscernibles. A thing is the sum of its properties. Two things are different only if they differ in at least one property. If two things have all of the same properties, then they are not different things. If there is no way at all to tell them apart, then they are the same thing.

Leibniz says to take the universe and switch east to west and west to east. The way contemporary philosophers set up the thought experiment is to use translation instead of reflection, but it is the same argument: Take the entire contents of the universe and shift it all three feet to the right. Is it any different?

Leibniz says no. The universe's history and future, every single event, and every single geometric and physical relation are all the same. The universe here and the shifted universe are indiscernible. Therefore, they are identical. If the original and shifted universe are the same universe, then there can't be a real space underneath, or else they would not be identical. Things would be at different real locations. These arguments did not convince either of the competitors.

Ernst Mach and Albert Einstein

At the end of the 19th century, the Austrian physicist Ernst Mach sought to create a worldview based entirely on science. He called it positivism, and it held as a fundamental postulate that the only things we should say exist are things we observe.

One person who read and was deeply influenced by both Mach and Leibniz was Albert Einstein. He thought they were right about space, and their direct influence on the development of the theory of relativity is obvious. The theory of relativity was first proposed by Einstein in his 1905 paper "On the Electrodynamics of Moving Bodies." In this paper, one of his interests is undermining the belief in the existence of a luminiferous aether—that is, an electromagnetic version of Newton's absolute space.

Einstein starts the paper with a thought argument. Moving a magnet back and forth through the coil causes an electric current to be generated. Moving the coil while keeping the magnet still produces the same results. It doesn't matter which one is moving as long as the rate is the same.

However, the classical explanations are different. When the magnet is moved, the current is the result of a changing magnetic field. When the coil is moved, it is the result of motion in a static magnetic field. The two, Einstein argues, are just different descriptions of the same physical situation.

If the physical situation is the same, then there is no underlying absolute truth about motion relative to the underlying electromagnetic space. There is no absolute space, only relative space. The original theory of relativity, what we call the special theory of relativity, justifies Leibniz's and Mach's relationism. The most famous result of the theory of special relativity was the equation $E = mc^2$, according to which mass becomes like heat or motion: another form of energy.

A New Theory

Einstein was not satisfied with special relativity for two reasons. First, the relative motion that it accounts for is limited, as it does not account for acceleration. Second, the theory includes mentions of every single force known in the universe except gravity. Einstein needed to generalize the theory of relativity in a fashion that accounted for acceleration and gravitation.

Ultimately, in 1916, the general theory of relativity came about. The general theory of relativity replaced Newton's old view, according to which gravity is a force between any two massive objects that are separated in space. According to Newton, mass is absolute, and distance is absolute, so the force of gravitation across space is absolutely determinable. The force travels across space, but it is not influenced by space.

However, Einstein saw space as sagging and warping with the weight of the stuff on it, changing its shape in a way that can cause things to change how they move. Space, in the general theory, is dynamic and interactive. This difference between Newton and Einstein involved flat versus curved space, and it gave rise to conflicting predictions in observable circumstances. The observations were carried out, and Einstein's predictions proved to be correct. This leads to the conclusion that on the basis of observable evidence, space is curved.

The philosophical ramifications are important: If we say that space is curved, then we are saying that space has the geometric property of being curved. A thing is defined by its properties. If we are attributing to space the property of being curved, then space has a property. To have a property means that it is a thing. Einstein's general theory of relativity seems to entail, contrary to Leibniz and Mach, that space is real. Space exists. Where the special theory of relativity seems to support Leibniz's relationism, the general theory of relativity seems to support Newton's substantivalism.

The Logical Positivists

The logical positivists were not so quick in the face of the new version of relativity theory to adopt a substantivalist viewpoint. They still thought that space is not a real thing unto itself. Their argument reached back to the French mathematician, physicist, and philosopher Henri Poincaré.

Poincaré argued that physics presupposes a geometry and that geometry presupposes a physics. It is a circle that is impossible to get out of scientifically. It is necessary to define one's way out by picking physics or geometry.

If you pick a geometry, then you can empirically develop a physics. Pick a physics, and geometry becomes an empirical science. The choice is free. It is a mere definition that we impose on the world, not something we learn from the world.

Hans Reichenbach

The logical empiricist Hans Reichenbach adapted Poincaré's argument to Einstein's new theory. Einstein says that gravitation is not a field in space like Newton thought but the curvature of space. Reichenbach argued we could think of the curvature itself as a field.

This raised the question of which field is desired. Do we want a flat space with a gravitational field that shrinks objects or a curved space with a gravitational field that does not? To determine if this question matters, Reichenbach reaches for Leibniz's principle of the identity of indiscernibles again. There is no difference between the two, so the two are not different.

The decision is not something that tells us how the world is. Rather, it determines how we go about linguistically describing it. The issue of curved versus flat space is not about a real property. If it is not a real property, then space is not a real thing. This rescues Leibniz and Mach's relationism.

Responses to Reichenbach

Some contemporary thinkers have sought to undermine the conventionalist approach, arguing that even though the curved space theory and the flat space theory give the same predictions, there is still philosophical reason to prefer the curved space version. That means that we should attribute a geometric property to space and hence hold that space exists as a thing.

Clark Glymour and Michael Friedman, for example, contend that we should buy into the idea that space is real, even though there are flat and curved space theories that make all the same predictions. The grounds they cite are various versions of Occam's razor. Occam's razor is the principle that when faced with two alternative theories, we ought to prefer the simplest one—that is, the one that posits the fewest entities.

Because saying something exists is an assumption, and assumptions can be wrong, we are least likely to be wrong when we make the fewest assumptions. Theories that employ the fewest entities as real are preferable.

Different philosophers have made this case in different ways. Friedman wrote the book *Foundations of Space-time Theories: Relativistic Physics and Philosophy of Science*. In this book, Friedman axiomatizes the theories of relativity—that is, he comes up with the most elegant set of basic sentences that allows us to describe the content of the special and general relativity.

This allows the comparison of the curved and flat versions of the general theory of relativity. The curved version has one fewer axiom. The reason for this is that Einstein creates the curved space by combining two elements: the curvature tensor that describes the geometry of space and the gravitational field. This results in one fewer element, and thus we need one fewer axiom. By Occam's razor, then, we should prefer the curved version. Space has a property, and so space is real.

Pro-Relationism Arguments

Others have offered arguments on the other side, maintaining that even though there seem to be actual claims about the geometry of space in general relativity, we should nonetheless maintain a relationism like Leibniz. This is the view of John Earman, John Norton, and John Stachel. Their attack on substantivalism derives from a historical quandary Einstein himself had to overcome in developing the general theory of relativity, the so-called hole argument.

The argument begins by positing the existence of a universe that is perfectly described by Einstein's theory. Every event that occurs is perfectly accounted for using general relativity. In this universe, the argument asks us to imagine a hole—that is, a small volume of space, far away from everything else.

The hole is a region of space completely free of any occurrences. There are no particles to bounce off of each other. Inside of this hole, they show, it is possible to take the geometry and twist it, thereby changing the gravitational field values inside but keeping them the same on the surface of the hole and in the rest of the universe.

The equations of the theory, they argue, would account for the twisted hole in exactly the same way as it does the non-twisted hole. Because the hole is empty, there is nothing different to explain. However, the substantivalists argue that the explanation necessarily attributes a specific, fixed geometry to space, and this property forces us to consider space to be a real thing. The property that is supposed to give us a reason to think space is real is its shape, its geometry.

The twisted and untwisted holes produce two different geometries equally well described by the same output of a single theory. The theory does not uniquely and completely determine the geometry of absolutely all of space. There seems to be no reason to attribute the geometric property to the space.

However, if space is not forced to have a shape, then it is not forced to have a property, and we are not forced to think it real. Substantivalism makes an extra, unnecessary, metaphysical claim. In this view, Occam's razor therefore does not force us to think that space is real. To the contrary, it forces us to reject the reality of space.

The Curved and Flat Versions of the General Theory of Relativity

C_1: $R_{jk} - \frac{1}{2} g_{jk} R = -8\pi\kappa T_{jk}$ $\qquad$ F_1: $R_{jk} - \frac{1}{2} g_{jk} R = -8\pi\kappa T_{jk}$

C_2: $g_{ij;k} = 0$ $\qquad$ F_2: $g_{ij;k} = 0$

C_3: $\frac{d^2 x_i}{d\tau^2} + \Gamma^i_{jk} \frac{dx_j}{d\tau} \frac{dx_k}{d\tau} = 0$ $\qquad$ F_3: $\frac{d^2 x_i}{d\tau^2} + \Gamma^i_{jk} \frac{dx_j}{d\tau} \frac{dx_k}{d\tau} = 0$

$\qquad\qquad\qquad\qquad\qquad\qquad$ F_4: $x_{ij} = 0$

Suggested Reading

Einstein, *Relativity*.
Huggett, *Space from Zeno to Einstein*.
Reichenbach, *The Philosophy of Space and Time*.

QUIZ QUESTIONS

1. Between Newton and Leibniz, who is the substantivalist and who is the relationist?

2. Mach says that only the person on the roller coaster feels sick after the ride because of:

    A. The Earth's magnetic field.
    B. The heat of the Sun.
    C. The motion of the roller coaster relative to the Earth.
    D. The motion of the roller coaster relative to the stars in the galaxy.

3. Which version of the theory of relativity includes gravitation, the special or general?

4. True or false: Poincaré held that there is a single unique geometry of space that can be experimentally determined with certainty.

5. Norton and Earman's hole argument involves a hole—that is, a region of space that includes no:

    A. Matter or energy.
    B. Light.
    C. Space.
    D. Gravity.

ANSWERS KEY CAN BE FOUND ON PAGE 118

THE NATURE OF EINSTEIN'S TIME

LECTURE 5

This lecture begins this course's look at the philosophical questions that arise from the nature of time. There are three main questions to consider. One is the direction of time: Why is the past unlike the future? The second is time travel: Are we stuck surfing the wave of time, or is it possible to swim through it? The third is the origin of time: Was there a start to time, and what came before that? This lecture will consider the first two questions, and the next lecture considers the third question.

Isaac Newton's Views

The verb we most naturally use in describing our commonsense view of time is *flow*. For example, consider this sentence: "Time flows like a mighty river." This is Isaac Newton's view. Just like his picture of absolute space, Newton also thought there was absolute time.

There is relative time—that is, how many ticks of the clock have passed or how many times the Sun has risen. But these are not real time. According to Newton, time, like space, is a thing unto itself, with a nature and properties. One of those properties is that it flows.

Flowing is directional. Earlier and later are different. The future and the past seem to be completely different. We can remember the past, but not the future. We can change the future, but not the past. According to Newton, this is because of the nature of time. Newton's laws of motion are not time directional. His laws work if the direction of time is reversed.

Hans Reichenbach's Views

Hans Reichenbach, the leader of the logical empiricists in Berlin, pointed out in his book *The Arrow of Time* that there is one place where we see time directionality: thermodynamics, the physics of heat. If one were to show a movie of a person kicking a football, it would obey the laws of mechanics both forward and backward.

Now imagine a movie of someone toasting a piece of bread. Toasting is an irreversible reaction. If a person takes a piece of bread and sticks it in the toaster, then puts it in the freezer, the result is not the original piece of bread but frozen toast. This is an asymmetry in physics, but it is also strange. Heat, after all, is just motion.

The 19th-century British physicist James Clerk Maxwell gave us the kinetic theory of heat. Matter, he argued, is made up of molecules. Those molecules are in motion. The temperature of a thing is just a measure of the average energy of motion—kinetic energy—of those molecules.

This motion should follow the mechanics of Newton or Einstein. Those are both time reversible. In the movie of someone toasting bread, upon close examination, it is the same movie as someone kicking a football, but with extremely small footballs instead. The size should not matter. The system obeys the same fundamental laws, and those laws are time reversible. Frozen toast should be impossible.

A Chemical Reaction and an Objection

An important consideration here is that the toasting of bread is a chemical reaction, not just a physical one. Among other things, there are bonds between molecules that change, but the idea is that there do seem to be processes that are nonreversible—that is, they pick out a direction of time. One place in thermodynamics where this is embodied, Reichenbach points out, is the infamous second law of thermodynamics. The second law does not say that the universe always becomes increasingly disordered but that entropy—a measure of the number of possible states—always increases.

Reichenbach argues that this tendency for entropy to increase could be seen to differentiate future from past because decreasing entropy requires actions that have effects. Cause-and-effect relations also seem to have a preferred direction. Causes have to come before effects. We should be able to follow the causal chains to see the privileged direction of time.

Objecting to this line is Huw Price in his book *Time's Arrow and Archimedes' Point*. Price contends that the sort of cause-based entropy argument Reichenbach advances doesn't work. To answer the question of the direction of time, Reichenbach thinks we need to answer the question of why entropy increases.

However, entropy is normal. There usually isn't a need to explain normal states of being. Rather, people usually try to explain the abnormal. High entropy is normal; order is abnormal. The thing we need to explain is not the increasing disorder, but what happened to make it ordered to begin with. The real question of time's direction hinges on an explanation of the order of the early universe.

The universe is expanding, and it used to have fewer possible states. In such a universe, entropy is increasing. However, if there is enough matter in the universe, the force of gravitation would be strong enough to stop the expansion and cause a universal contraction.

This shrinking of the universe would limit the number of possible states things could be in. In other words, this empirical possibility could very well lead to a universe where entropy tends to decrease. This means that we cannot rely on entropy if we are looking for an intrinsically time directional basis in physics.

Back to the Start

Physics has made it perfectly possible that entropy would be incapable of doing what we need it to do. This brings this lecture's first question back to its starting point: Why should we think that time flows in one special direction? Should we even believe it flows at all?

The philosopher John McTaggart Ellis McTaggart is best remembered for his distinction between two conceptions of time which he sets out in his famous article "The Unreality of Time."

McTaggart labels these A-time and B-time. In A-time, we are fixed observers with time flowing past us. A-time has three metaphysically different realms. There is the past: moments that are fixed and gone. There is the present, which is now and experienced. And there is the future, which is open and has not yet come to be.

In B-time, on the other hand, time is fixed, and we move through it. History is an interconnected block of unchanging temporal relations. The future is just as fixed as the past. Time doesn't change; human consciousness does. We only remember the past, not the future.

The two are incompatible, although McTaggart argues that aspects of both are essential to any successful philosophical account of time. As such, he concludes, the notion of time is self-contradictory, and thus time is an illusion.

Relativity and Time Dilation

While McTaggart's distinction was in no way influenced by Einstein, it is necessary to add relativity to the discussion because there are a couple of interesting temporal effects. These will lead to the question of time travel.

Here, a relevant effect is called time dilation. Time passes at different rates for different observers moving at different speeds. It was most colorfully illustrated by Albert Einstein's friend, the French physicist Paul Langevin, with his infamous twins paradox. Imagine two twins who are both 20 years old. One stays on Earth while the other becomes an astronaut.

The astronaut travels very fast for the duration of the mission, returning to the planet 20 years later. The twin on Earth will be 20 years older—that is, 40 years old. The twin stepping out of the rocket will only be 37 years old. The astronaut twin would have only experienced 17 years in the time the Earth-bound twin experienced 20. The passing of time is a relative measure.

Einstein understood this, but he did not, however, fully understand the philosophically radical nature of the insight. After he published on it, the paper was read by a mathematician-turned-physicist named Hermann Minkowski who did understand exactly how radical it was.

Minkowski recast the theory: No longer can space and time be thought of as independent elements, as Newton conceived. Rather, they had to be thought of as united into a single four-dimensional space-time. This initially angered Einstein.

However, eventually he settled down and realized how important Minkowski's work was. By explaining the theory geometrically, Minkowski showed the interrelation of space and time. This is what Einstein needed to develop the general theory of relativity, in which gravitation is understood geometrically.

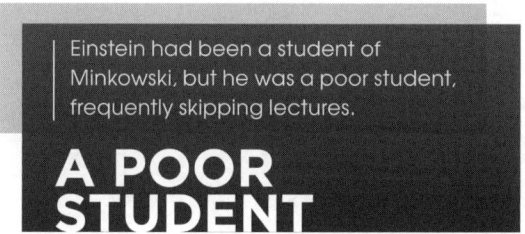

Einstein had been a student of Minkowski, but he was a poor student, frequently skipping lectures.

A POOR STUDENT

Four-Dimensional Beings

Note that gravitation is understood as the curvature of space. However, as Minkowski showed, space and time are not independent, and it is space-time that warps.

We are four-dimensional beings. In space-time, we are like veins flowing through a mollusk. From the four-dimensional perspective of space-time, each of us is a tube worming its way through.

One person who understood this was the Austrian mathematician Kurt Gödel. He recognized that we are all just tubes in a squishy mollusk. He wanted to think about how strange a shape we could make by squeezing the mollusk.

Gödel showed that if one set up matter and energy in just the right alignment and had an electron moving fast enough, one could get the space-time to warp so radically that the electron would bounce off of its earlier self. It would collide with itself. Einstein's general theory of relativity predicts the possibility of time travel. This opens the door to time machines, and that leads to the paradoxes of time travel.

Suggested Reading

Lewis, "The Paradoxes of Time Travel."
Price, *Time's Arrow and Archmedes' Point*.
Reichenbach, *The Direction of Time*.

LECTURE 5 ◀ The Nature of Einstein's Time

QUIZ QUESTIONS

1. According to Newton, is the time it takes the Earth to go around the Sun a measure or absolute or relative time?

2. True or false: Newton's laws work if time flows either forward or backward.

3. What field of physics does Reichenbach cite as giving time directional laws?

    A. Mechanics
    B. Optics
    C. Gravitation
    D. Thermodynamics

4. In which of McTaggart's models of time, A-time or B-time, does time flow?

5. True or false: Price argues that the universe could change so that entropy tends to decrease.

ANSWERS KEY CAN BE FOUND ON PAGE 118

THE BEGINNING OF TIME

LECTURE 6

Events seem to happen in a linear order. However, there are questions about time related to philosophy and physics: How far back does it go? Did time start? This lecture looks at how different thinkers have approached such questions.

Early Thinkers

Determining if and when time started was not a task for the ancient Greeks. Aristotle, for example, gives us a universe with no temporal origin. The universe works as it always has.

Matters changed when Judeo-Christian thinkers came to the question with the theological need for a temporal origin. Saint Thomas Aquinas adored Aristotle, but he realized that certain elements in Aristotle's work would need tweaking if they were to fit with Aquinas's theological commitments.

In his masterwork *Summa Theologica*, Aquinas both adopts and adapts Aristotle's argument to contend that God is the prime mover and thereby the initial cause of the universe. There must have been, he argues, a beginning to time.

The Move to Science

It took 500 years for the issue to move from theology to physics. It arrived there by mistake. In 1916, Albert Einstein put the finishing touches on the general theory of relativity. The heart of the theory are the Einstein field equations, which specify the way space-time must behave given the distribution of matter and energy within it.

In considering some of the easier models to work through, the Belgian physicist and Catholic priest Georges Lemaître realized something strange. They weren't stable. Except for a split second, every single model would be constantly expanding or contracting.

The theory had to be fixed. Einstein added a single new term: the cosmological constant. Its job was to add a force to the universe that affects the universe as a whole by pulling or pushing in a way that counteracts the problematic expansion or contraction. That occurred in 1917. In 1931, Edwin Hubble produced experimental evidence that the universe was expanding. The theory had been right.

> Hubble's evidence that the universe was expanding was based on the fact that almost everything in the sky looked redder than it really was. As something moves closer, it looks bluer. As something moves away, it looks redder.

HUBBLE'S EVIDENCE

Looking for a Cause

If the universe is expanding, that means it had to have been smaller in the past, and there had to be something causing the expansion. There is only one force that operates with sufficient force over long distances: gravitation. Gravitation's only direction is attraction. Gravity could slow that expansion down as things pull on each other, but expansion requires a push, not a pull. Gravity could not cause the expansion, although it could stop it by generating enough pull.

This led to the question of the end of time. If the universe is expanding, there is less and less energy per unit volume. Eventually, if the universe expanded enough, that amount of energy would be insufficient to sustain any sort of interesting phenomena, including life.

However, if there was enough gravitational pull, then the gravitational brake would stop the expansion and cause a contraction. Gravitation would give rise to a universe accelerating inward that would collapse in on itself. It would concentrate its energy into greater and greater amounts per unit volume until it became too hot to sustain atoms or nuclei.

Perhaps, when the energy was sufficiently high, it would trigger some mechanism we don't know about and cause the universe to expand again. Those seemed to be the only three possibilities. It all depended on what the critical mass would have to be to cause a massive crunch. This necessitated the weighing of everything to see if there was at least that much substance in the universe.

When it came to weighing everything, a problem arose for researchers: There was something in the universe they couldn't see. This is called dark matter. It is the excess weight in the universe.

Another task was to measure how much the universe was slowing down. However, it wasn't slowing down its expansion at all. It was actually speeding up. Gravity is only capable of slowing down the expansion. There is some other force, which is known as dark energy.

Theories on Expansion

In the 1940s, there were two theories on what initially caused the universe's expansion. One sought to maintain a temporal version of the Copernicus principle—that is, the past should look like the present, which should look like the future. There was never a unique cosmic event and never will be. This is called the steady-state theory and was developed by Fred Hoyle, Thomas Gold, and Hermann Bondi.

A competing theory developed by George Gamow held that the past did not look like the present. If things are getting bigger now, then they must have been smaller in the past, and something must have caused them to expand. This became known as the big-bang theory.

The case was settled by accident. At Bell Labs in New Jersey, two researchers received a hand-me-down radio telescope from the government. The researchers were Arno Penzias and Robert Wilson. They prepared to use their new tool and set about calibrating the telescope, but to their frustration, they found that there was some background noise they couldn't seem to get rid of.

Thirty miles away at Princeton University, physicist Robert Dicke realized that one of the differences between the steady-state and the big-bang theories was testable. If the big-bang theory was right, then there ought to be a background radiation, an energy fingerprint left everywhere in the universe. He and some colleagues did the work to calculate what it should be and came to a figure. To look for it, they would need a radio telescope.

When Penzias and Wilson told a colleague about their problem with the background noise, the friend told them about a paper he had read from Princeton that wasn't published yet. The paper was about constant, ever-present background radiation that should be everywhere.

After reading it, they invited Dicke out to Bell Labs to see their setup and examine their data. In a gesture of generous cooperation, they both published their papers together as back-to-back articles in the same journal. Dicke and his team published their theoretical calculation, and then Penzias and Wilson published their data confirming the calculation.

The big-bang theory was experimentally verified. It won the battle with the steady-state theory.

Philosophy and the Big Bang

The big bang itself is a philosophically interesting issue. What does it mean to have a scientifically validated theory that postulates a big bang, a seeming origin of time itself?

Pope Pius XII contended that it means that science has been able to provide empirical evidence for the existence of the Christian creator God. He held that the confirmation of the big bang theory was not only consistent with the theological notion of creation from nothing but leads to it. The big-bang theory uses science to get us back to the instant when God created the universe.

This interpretation of big-bang cosmology is opposed by one of the giants of 20th-century philosophy of physics, Adolf Grünbaum. He turned his talents to the claim that the big-bang theory validates the biblical account of creation in the article "The Pseudo-Problem of Creation in Physical Cosmology." The term *pseudo-problem* comes from the logical positivists. The idea is that there are real questions, and these demand our attention. Pseudo-questions, meanwhile, look like questions but are not questions.

A question is a request for information. If the information requested does not exist, then there is no real question. For example, asking a person what color their sister's car is would be a pseudo-question if the person does not have a sister. That is exactly the status Grünbaum assigns to seeming questions, such as: What happened before the big bang? What caused the big bang?

Those contending that big-bang cosmology provides good reason to believe in creation are, he argues, committing at least one of three sorts of fallacies. The first logical error is the inference that is made when it is asserted that because everything is caused, there must be a cause of the universe. In the premise that everything is caused, we are looking for causes within the universe. For instance, it is reasonable to ask why items are in a grocery store, but it does not follow that creation of things in the grocery store entails creation from nothing by the will of a supernatural being.

The second group of reasoning errors that Grünbaum points to are questions like this: What happened before the big bang? However, to ask what happened in the time before time is self-contradictory. It seems to make sense when we come from a place of classical time, but not if we realize that we are talking here about the origin of time itself.

Finally, Grünbaum claims that science can only give answers that the human mind can comprehend. God is beyond the comprehension of the human mind and therefore beyond the reach of science. Science gets us to the big bang, but faith gets us the rest of the way to the divine.

Grünbaum argues that if a belief is beyond science because it is beyond human comprehension, then it must also be beyond faith. One can only have faith in a proposition one understands. If something is beyond the scope of science to obtain evidence because it is beyond our comprehension, then it is also beyond our ability to believe on the basis of faith.

Take away these three moves and, Grünbaum argues, the arguments that big-bang cosmology leads to divine creation go away, too. It is interesting to consider whether or not he is correct. Philosophy deals with the big questions, but philosophy of cosmology deals with the biggest ones of all.

Suggested Reading

Boslough, *Masters of Time*.
Ferris, *Coming of Age in the Milky Way*.
Leslie, *Modern Cosmology and Philosophy*.

QUIZ QUESTIONS

1. According to Aristotle, all astronomical bodies are made up of what element?

   A. Earth.
   B. Water.
   C. Air.
   D. Fire.
   E. Aether.

2. True or false: According to Aquinas, time has no beginning.

3. What astronomer detected the red shift of virtually all galaxies we observe?

4. Penzias and Wilson's accidental discovery of the cosmic background radiation supplies supporting evidence for what theory?

5. A pseudo-question has no:

   A. Sense.
   B. Answer.
   C. Words.
   D. Punctuation.

ANSWERS KEY CAN BE FOUND ON PAGE 118

ARE ATOMS REAL?

LECTURE 7

This lecture examines the following question: Why should we believe in the existence of atoms? The question about the nature of matter has been a fundamental issue since classical times, and we have great confidence in the atomic hypothesis. Is such confidence warranted, and even if it is, should the theory be literally interpreted?

The Atomic Hypothesis

The atomic hypothesis well predates contemporary physics. In classical Greece, thinkers such as Democritus and Epicurus argued that matter was composed of basic particles—that is, atoms. The word *atom* means "uncuttable" because they would be the smallest part of all material things.

By the 16th and 17th centuries, thinking had changed. Atoms at that time smacked of naïve metaphysics that authentic science was seeking to overcome in being truly rational. To speak about uncuttable, invisible particles was embarrassing in a scientific context.

However, atoms went from an embarrassing, childish metaphysical fantasy of speculative philosophers to an accepted truth in the hardest of the hard sciences. The evidence behind that shift came from two different directions: physics and chemistry.

The evidence from the physics side came from the study of the physics of materials, especially gases. Thermodynamics examines how properties of heated bodies behave. The idea that heated bodies were just made up of tiny little bodies in motion appealed to physicists because it made all chemistry a branch of physics.

In the 1730s, Daniel Bernoulli first proposed the idea of a kinetic theory of heat—that is, the idea that heat was just a result of motion. It slowly gained momentum with physicists, but the chemists disliked it, in part because it diminished chemistry.

Examining Heat

Chemistry was the science of substances. Heat was long thought to be not a property of substances but instead a substance itself. Many classical views of the nature of matter classified heat, or fire, as a basic substance. Aristotle's worldview did, and as Aristotle became the official doctrine of the Catholic Church, most European scientists did as well.

An important concept early on was that of phlogiston. When Joseph Priestley discovered oxygen in the 1770s, he thought that it was dephlogisticated air. Air was a substance, and heat was a substance. Removing heat from air created a new, pure substance. Air without phlogiston could do lots of interesting things. Putting a glass jar over a burning piece of paper would cause the paper to stop burning. Adding dephlogisticated air would cause the flame to come roaring back. The air inside of the jar had reached its full phlogiston capacity and could not take any more out of the paper. The phlogiston flow—that is, the flame—stopped. Adding dephlogisticated air allowed more phlogiston to flow out, bringing the return of the flame.

Around the same time, Antoine-Laurent Lavoisier was thinking differently about that sort of experiment. He re-ran Priestley's experiments with burning paper and dephlogisticated air, and he found that the ashes of the burned paper were heavier than the unburned paper. Phlogiston theory said that the fire of the burning paper was the paper giving off phlogiston. How could something giving off a substance end up heavier than when it had it?

One possible explanation is that phlogiston has negative mass. However, it seemed more likely that something was being added to the paper in the process of burning. Lavoisier formulated the principle of the conservation of mass—that mass could neither be created nor destroyed—and concluded that the gas was adding something to the paper in the process of burning. That something would turn out to be oxygen.

Priestley and others were starting to find different gases that had different properties. It became difficult to keep up with the different sorts of air that were being created through various chemical means. Another factor was Lavoisier's undermining of phlogiston theory. Air was no longer a single substance, and heat was not a substance at all. Suddenly, the questions began to multiply for the chemists. The different versions of air were created from different reactions with different chemicals.

The Early 1800s

In the early 1800s, Joseph Louis Proust and John Dalton noticed that the recipes used to create the different chemical reactions had an interesting property: They required amounts of substances in simple proportions. For example, taking hydrogen and oxygen, running electricity through them, and producing water would take twice as much hydrogen as oxygen. Any more hydrogen would not convert and be left over.

The ultimate number related to all these substances was derived by Lorenzo Romano Amedeo Carlo Avogadro. His great discovery was that if one held the pressure and temperature constant, then the mass of the gas would be directly proportional to the volume. If the atomic hypothesis were true, then this fact could be used to determine the relative molecular weights of the molecules of the gas.

It also followed that at a standard pressure, temperature, and volume, there would be a specific number of molecules. It would be called a mole of the substance. The number itself would be known as Avogadro's number, which is approximately 6.022×10^{23}.

Molecules

In the 1860s, James Clerk Maxwell had a series of papers designed to show that matter was comprised of what he called molecules. He starts from the assumption that gases are made of molecules. He further assumes that these molecules are perfectly spherical, infinitely hard, and interact only through contact. They are purely mechanical with no electrical charges.

If temperature is a measure of the kinetic energy of those particles and pressure is the result of the force of collisions with the container, then Maxwell showed that the behavior of the collection of these tiny little billiard balls is exactly what we observe in the behavior of gases. If we take gases to be made up of molecules, hypothetically, then they would have to behave almost exactly the way we know real gases to actually behave

He assumed the molecules were perfectly spherical, infinitely hard, and not electrically charged to make the mathematics manageable. He knew that these assumptions were false. Real molecules would not be like this sort of idealization. That is why it is called the ideal gas law. It holds exactly only for ideal gases, and it is $PV = nRT$.

P, V, and T—pressure, volume, and temperature—are measurable macroscopic properties. R is a number—that is, a constant to make the units come out correctly. However, n is the number of microscopic entities. This law connects the empirically observable macroscopic world with the invisible, theoretical, hypothetical microscopic world. Still, many were unconvinced.

Einstein and Perrin

Then in 1905, along came Einstein. In one of five papers he wrote that year that changed the world, Einstein worked with statistical reasoning to show that he could explain the strange effect known as Brownian motion. Discovered by Robert Brown, the idea is that if small particles of, for example, dust, are suspended in liquid, they move. They do not move smoothly. They move randomly. Particles near each other would exhibit completely different motions. The question was what caused this.

Some had suggested that it was the collisions of the molecules of the water hitting the dust particles. However, Einstein realized that it wasn't individual molecules but a constant barrage. He showed that if the water were made up of molecules whose speed was dependent on the temperature, then it was possible to calculate odds of a force imbalance that would cause the random zigzagging we see. He derived observable results, at least in principle. Jean Perrin put this into practice. In 1913, Perrin did the experimental work, and it turned out that Einstein's calculations were right on target. The combination of Einstein's theory and Perrin's experiment is widely held to be the final blow that nailed down the existence of atoms.

A NOBEL PRIZE WINNER

For his work in helping to prove the existence of atoms, Perrin was awarded the Nobel Prize.

Should We Believe?

How we came to believe in atoms is a matter of history. The question of whether we should believe it is a matter of philosophy. Philosophy of physics launched with the logical positivists, and the figure at the vanguard of the logical positivist movement was Rudolf Carnap.

One of the goals of logical positivism was to clean up the human belief structure. They sought to remove everything that wasn't directly observed. Carnap proposed doing this by limiting the language of science to that based on direct observations.

Atoms were a significant problem for Carnap. There does not seem to be a way to build the notion of an atom as we use it in physics out of basic observation reports. The concept comes out of our scientific theories, and we want rational belief to be guided by scientific theories that are well supported by evidence.

However, there is not a straightforward way of making sense of these theoretical terms. Theoretical terms are those parts of the theory that are not directly measurable. They are still needed as part of a scientific theory.

Carnap wanted to eliminate metaphysics, replacing it entirely with empirical science and logic. To his chagrin, science seemed to keep on reintroducing metaphysics, foiling the plan. The conundrum, especially with respect to atoms, led some of the younger logical positivists and students who had been drawn to the logical positivists to begin to part ways. A new movement arose that sought to put metaphysics back into human knowledge under the condition that it came in through science.

Scientific Realism

This new movement is called scientific realism. It is made up of two important components. The first is the idea that we ought to interpret our best theories as probably true—that is, descriptive of the world. The second is the idea that theoretical terms in those theories are part of the furniture of the world: If a central term is essential to one of our best theories, we ought to think it is real even if it is unobservable.

The first condition was clearly problematic because everyone wanted to hold that science progresses. Our best theories now will, no doubt, be replaced with new, better theories eventually. This raises a question: How can we hold science to give us truth—the central element in scientific realism—if we know all theories are born false, just a link in a chain?

We hold the best theory at any given moment to be approaching truth. With each new step, we move closer to having truth. It is an asymptotic process in which each new best theory is approximately true.

The second element—that the machinery of the best current theory should be thought to reflect the actual constituents of reality—is called entity realism. Our best theory of matter employs atoms in it, so we should believe that atoms exist.

One of the leading figures in scientific realism was the Australian philosopher J. J. C. Smart. Smart argues that we might be able to logically do what Carnap wanted to do in eliminating all non-observable entities from our best scientific theories.

In his view, atoms are the mechanism that explains the observed relations of macroscopic properties. To believe in the laws that Maxwell derived without believing in the microscopic entities he used in the derivation would be to believe in what he called a cosmic coincidence.

Opposition

In opposition to scientific realism, Bas van Fraassen offers a different picture of science, which he calls constructive empiricism. In his book *The Scientific Image*, van Fraassen contends that while the positivists went too far, so too did the scientific realists. There is a tension between empiricism—that we ought to derive all of our views about the world from observation—and metaphysics—that we can say something about what is real in the world. Carnap's project did not work, but that does not mean that we surrender to the new metaphysicians.

Van Fraassen starts by saying that we want to accept our best theories. He says that he accepts atomic theory. He also contends that all we are doing in accepting the theory is agreeing that it is empirically adequate—that is, we believe that everything observable that the theory predicts is or will be observed.

The function of physics is not to pull back the curtain on the invisible inner workings of reality. It is much more modest. The function is to give us good tools to make predictions and organize our knowledge. When we accept a theory, we are saying it is a good tool. It does its job. If we ask our theories to do too much, if we ask them to tell us exactly what the invisible world really looks like, then we risk going too far and telling the invisible world how it has to be.

Suggested Reading

Perrin, *Atoms*.
Pullman, *The Atom in the History of Human Thought*.
Smart, *Philosophy and Scientific Realism*.

LECTURE 7 ◂ Are Atoms Real?

QUIZ QUESTIONS

1. Which of the following Greek thinkers was an atomist?

    A. Aristotle.
    B. Plato.
    C. Socrates.
    D. Democritus.
    E. Parmenides.

2. True or false: The kinetic theory of heat equates heat with motion.

3. The flowing heat substance hypothesized in the 18th century was called what?

4. Logical positivists take protocol sentences to be the building blocks of all human knowledge because they are:

    A. Observable.
    B. Logical.
    C. Imaginable.
    D. Fictional.

5. True or false: Smart believes that atoms are just mental constructs that are useful but are not really parts of the universe.

ANSWERS KEY CAN BE FOUND ON PAGE 118

QUANTUM STATES: NEITHER TRUE NOR FALSE?

LECTURE 8

Before quantum mechanics, physical theories were what philosophers call deterministic. Determinism means that what comes before fully determines what comes after. However, then came quantum mechanics. This lecture looks at what quantum mechanics is and where it came from.

The End of the 19th Century

At the end of the 19th century, Newton's theory of mechanics and gravitation and Maxwell's theory of electricity, magnetism, and light led people to believe that almost everything was accounted for. There were a couple of strange phenomena we had to figure out, but that would soon be done, and physics would be complete. One of those led to relativity, but a couple of others led in a completely different direction. They were blackbody radiation and the photoelectric effect.

Blackbody Radiation

The problem of blackbody radiation can be imagined by thinking about a hollow metal sphere. If heated, it glows. Giving off light means getting rid of some of its energy. However, now imagine a hollow metal sphere with a black surface, meaning no energy is lost.

The inside will still glow, but the energy emitted inside the sphere will be reabsorbed by the sphere because it stays inside. This reabsorbed energy would further heat up the sphere, causing it to give off more energy inside that would be reabsorbed.

It seems like the energy inside of the sphere would reinforce itself, increasing to infinity. That doesn't work. The question was why not.

Max Planck, the biggest name in physics the generation before Einstein, decided to work the problem backward. He started from the actual data for energy at each wavelength of light for a given temperature to see what curve would fit.

A theory emerged, but it required a strange move. He could explain everything if light was emitted and absorbed only in packets. Everything worked out if one were to use the assumption that light was emitted and absorbed in energy packets of the size $E = h\nu$, where ν is the frequency of the light and h is a constant called Planck's constant. This makes the units and numbers come out correctly.

The amount of light that something gave off had to be $E = nh\nu$, where n is a counting number, such as 2 or 3. To make the theory fit the curve, light had to work like a lamp with a three-way bulb that could give off only specific amounts of light, with no amounts in between. Planck dismissed this as unreal but took it as necessary to make the math work.

The Photoelectric Effect

A second troubling phenomenon of this period was the photoelectric effect. It was found that shining ultraviolet light on metal causes electrons to be kicked out of the metal. The strange part was under the thinking of the time, brighter light should lead to electrons that come out faster. Increased energy in should entail increased energy out. However, that is not what happens. Brighter light results in more electrons, but they move as fast as they were with the dimmer light.

Einstein figured out a solution, but it required Planck's assertion that light is emitted and absorbed in packets. Think of the light not as a wave hitting the metal but as resembling tiny footballs. Making the light does not mean a larger wave shaking electrons free. Rather, it means more footballs banging against electrons, knocking them out of the surface.

Quantization and the Atom

Blackbody radiation and the photoelectric effect represent a pair of anomalous cases solved with the assumption of quantization. In this case, the term *quantum* refers to something that can be counted.

THE NUCLEUS

> For discovering the nucleus, Ernest Rutherford received a Nobel Prize in Chemistry.

Matters changed when Niels Bohr saw he had to make the same move with respect to the most basic element in the universe: atoms. The idea of small, light, negatively charged electrons and a small, dense nucleus of positive charge gave rise to the solar system model of the atom.

In this model, there are protons tightly packed into the nucleus and electrons moving around the nucleus at various distances. However, this can't be true. If electrons are negatively charged and moving around the nucleus, the atom would be unstable. This raised the question: How do we build stable atoms?

The answer, Bohr discovered, was to quantize energy. Electrons could only be in specific tracks around the nucleus. They could not orbit at any old distance. They could move from an inner track to an outer track if the atom took in exactly the right amount of energy. They could also do the opposite. However, they could never have been at the points in between the two tracks.

In the basic component of all matter, the smooth was becoming discrete. Electrons were moving in a way that couldn't be described by mechanics—that is, the theory of motion. A new mechanics that would account for this quantization was required. That—quantum mechanics—became the project for physics.

Bohr and Heisenberg

Bohr had an assistant, Werner Heisenberg, who figured out a way to take all the strange results that were coming out of atomic physics and structure them in a mathematical system. The trick, Heisenberg realized, was to generalize the notion of an observable property.

Usually, people use numbers to represent the value of a property; for example, the length of a bridge is 15 meters. The mass of the liquid was five grams. Other properties needed vectors—that is, ordered triples of numbers. Each number is for each perpendicular direction.

Heisenberg realized that to do quantum mechanics, a matrix—not a vector—is required. A matrix is a rectangular array of numbers or even a stack of rectangular arrays of numbers. Some of these stacks would require an infinite number of rectangular arrays of numbers. The math was now so difficult that it was nearly impossible to use.

Some of the matrices behaved strangely. For example, multiplication is supposed to be commutative. Changing the order of the numbers being multiplied will give the same result. However, Heisenberg realized that in quantum mechanics, there would be odd pairs of properties whose matrices did not follow the usual multiplication commutative relation. For position, there was momentum. For time, there was energy. It seemed they were tied together and couldn't be separated, but each was always trying to undermine the other.

This is the basis for what has become known as the Heisenberg uncertainty principle. There are pairs of physical properties such that observation of one—that is, the determination of parts of its matrix—disallows the determination of parts of the matrix of the other. Usually this comes up in terms of position and momentum. The idea is that the more exactly we determine the position to be, the less exact of a velocity a particle has. The same applies in the other direction: The more exactly we know the velocity, the less the thing actually has an exact position.

Erwin Schrödinger

The Austrian physicist Erwin Schrödinger did away with the need for infinite-dimensional matrices. Schrödinger came up with a simple second-order differential equation that turned out to be exactly equivalent to Heisenberg's matrix mechanics. The Schrödinger equation captured everything the matrices did, but it had the great virtue of being easy to use.

The Schrödinger equation is the state equation of the theory of quantum mechanics—that is, it is the equation that governs the state of a quantum system. State equations have state variables that show what the relevant properties of the system are. For Newtonian mechanics, the state equations are the equations of motion and the state variables are mass, position, velocity, and acceleration.

When examining a particle in a situation that has a certain potential energy associated with it, the Schrödinger equation can reveal some information about its position. The equation does not tell us where the particle is. It tells us where it could be and the likelihood we will find it there if we look. The uncertainty inherent in the theory is epistemological. It is about how much or little we can know about the properties that the system has.

Before we observe it, a particle is in the combination of all of the positions. This is called its state of superposition, or its superposed state. The Schrödinger equation is a law of nature. It does describe the state of the system, but we never see things in these superposed states. When we measure them, they always have one particular value for the property.

This is called the measurement problem. Before we perform a measurement, the particle is in its superposed state as dictated by the Schrödinger equation. When we look at it, the solution of the law of nature goes away, and the thing has a single, definite value of the property.

Why would a law of nature only hold for the universe when we don't look at it, but fail the instant we do? This allows us to fully account for the uncertainty Heisenberg discovered. When one solves the Schrödinger equation for a particle in a situation in terms of position, the result is a string of all the possible positions multiplied by probabilities. When done in terms of velocity, the result is a string of all the possible velocities, each multiplied by a measure of the probability. When its position is measured, the superposition collapses to a single value, but one cannot know which it will be.

Doing that puts the particle in the full superposition in terms of the non-commuting observable partner. Collapsing the solution in terms of position will expand it in terms of velocity. Collapsing it in terms of velocity will expand it in terms of position. The Schrödinger solutions are not uncertain, because things have values we don't know. The mathematical combination is the actual state.

Breaking Logic

This challenges common sense as well as logic. Classical logic going back to Aristotle was based on the principle of the excluded middle, which says that all sentences have one of two truth values: true or false.

Quantum mechanics demands that we give up that foundation for rational thought. Take this sentence: "The particle is at position 5." If, after observation, the particle is at position 5, the sentence is true. If it is not at position 5 after observation, the sentence is false. However, if one measures its velocity instead of its position, the particle will be in its superposed state with respect to the non-commuting observable position.

If it is in the superposed state of being spread out through all possible values probabilistically, is the sentence "The particle is at position 5" true or false? It is not quite true, but it is not quite false. Quantum mechanics broke logic.

Logic is the tool of the philosopher, so philosophers tried to fix it with a new logic for quantum mechanics. The person most associated with this project is John von Neumann. Neumann realized that we could possibly fix things with the addition of a new truth value to augment true and false. The new value is called indeterminate.

Figure 8.1

Consider the logical connective *or*. We traditionally define our logical notions using what we call truth-tables. This is a means of considering all possible situations. For *or*, the truth-table looks like **Figure 8.1**.

P	Q	P OR Q
T	T	T
T	F	T
F	T	T
F	F	F

Or connects two sentences called P and Q. An or-sentence is true when either of the sentences connected by *or* is true. For example, "Bob has sugar or cream in his coffee" is true if either Bob has sugar or Bob has cream in his coffee (or both). It would only be wrong if he had neither. That is why in the first row, true or true is true. In the second row, true or false is true. In the third row, false or true is true. And in the last row, false or false (no cream and no sugar) is the only false one.

LECTURE 8 ◂ Quantum States: Neither True nor False?

Adding the indeterminate truth value can make or-sentences become complicated. We no longer have just four possible cases. We now have nine possible cases to consider (**Figure 8.2**).

Figure 8.2

P	Q	P OR Q
T	T	
T	I	
T	F	
I	T	
I	I	
I	F	
F	T	
F	I	
F	F	

Filling in all the cases we know from the classical *or*, we get the truth-table shown in **Figure 8.3**.

Figure 8.3

P	Q	P OR Q
T	T	T
T	I	
T	F	T
I	T	
I	I	
I	F	
F	T	T
F	I	
F	F	F

We know that an or-sentence is true if either of the connected sentences is true, so that gives us the truth-table in **Figure 8.4**.

Figure 8.4

P	Q	P or Q
T	T	T
T	I	T
T	F	T
I	T	T
I	I	
I	F	
F	T	T
F	I	
F	F	F

Common sense tells us that indeterminate means it could be true, and it could be false. False or indeterminate means that it might be false or true, or it might be false or false. In the end, we don't know. Indeterminate or false and false or indeterminate should have the value I. This gives us the truth-table in **Figure 8.5**.

Figure 8.5

P	Q	P or Q
T	T	T
T	I	T
T	F	T
I	T	T
I	I	
I	F	I
F	T	T
F	I	I
F	F	F

There is just one spot left. Common sense tells us that the indications of indeterminate or indeterminate mean that either could be either, so surely that last one is also indeterminate.

However, this is quantum mechanics, so common sense does not necessarily apply. Suppose that we have a property that has only two possible values. One example is what physicists call spin. It has two possible values: up and down. If the particle we are considering is in its superposed state, and P is the sentence "This particle is spin up" and Q is the sentence "This particle is spin down," then both P and Q will have the truth-value I because the superposed state makes this indeterminate.

We know that the particle is either spin up or spin down—those are the only two possibilities. This raises the question: What do we know about the sentence P or Q in the case where both are indeterminate? It has to be true. That gives us the truth-table in **Figure 8.6**.

This is a strange logic that only became more complex the more von Neumann and those who followed worked on it. But if the world is that weird, then the reasonable way of thinking about it has to be weird as well.

Figure 8.6

P	Q	P OR Q
T	T	T
T	I	T
T	F	T
I	T	T
I	I	T
I	F	I
F	T	T
F	I	I
F	F	F

Suggested Reading

Jones, *The Quantum Ten.*
Lovett Cline, *Men Who Made a New Physics.*

QUIZ QUESTIONS

1. True or false: Blackbodies give off infinite energy.

2. Was Ernest Rutherford awarded the Nobel Prize in physics or chemistry for his discovery of the nucleus?

3. Who discovered that the simple solar system model of the atom was unstable because the rotating electron should spiral into the nucleus?

4. Whose equation replaced Heisenberg's matrix mechanics as the foundation of quantum mechanics?

5. How many truth values does classical logic have? How many does the quantum logic proposed by von Neumann have?

ANSWERS KEY CAN BE FOUND ON PAGE 118

WAVES, PARTICLES, AND QUANTUM ENTANGLEMENT

LECTURE 9

Physicists derive theories to answer questions. Those theories include three kinds of elements. One collection of elements are the empirical notions—that is, directly observable terms like mass and distance. A second is formalism—that is, parts of the mathematical grammar, like equal signs, needed to write out equations. The first group is meant to refer to the world. The second is not. Mass picks out a property of reality. The equal sign allows us to say things about reality.

Theoretical entities make up the third category. They include things like a gravitational field that is used but not actually seen. They are employed in the theory as more than just mathematical machinery, but they are not directly observable. They, or aspects of them, can be calculated using the empirical and mathematical elements, and they connect the theory in a way that gives us access to additional observable consequences—that is, predictions we can test.

They raise the deep philosophical question about theories in physics: What does it mean when the predictions of a theory are true? What does it mean to accept a theory? Does it mean that we are accepting that the theory is a literal accounting of the furniture and behavior of the world?

Two Groups

Philosophers tend to divide into two groups around such questions. Scientific realists hold theoretical terms to be like observational terms. The realist takes the unobservable parts of the theory and holds them to be unobservable parts of the world.

Empiricists, on the other hand, take the theoretical terms to be like the formal, grammatical parts of the theory. All that is real is what we can see, and the unobservable terms are simply contracted concepts that let us connect the real observable elements in new and clever ways.

At the beginning of the 20th century, the theoretical notion of the atom seemed to give a decisive victory to the realists over the empiricists. It may be true that no one had ever seen an atom, but atomic theory is so successful that it seemed absurd to consider atoms nothing more than a useful mental construct. Even in the face of the success of atomic theory, there remained some empiricists who wanted to deny the existence of atoms.

Quantum Mechanics

Atomic theory led to quantum mechanics, which is where matters become philosophically interesting. A notable figure here is Louis de Broglie. He realized that modern physics had two branches: relativity theory and quantum mechanics. Each has an iconic equation that represented its central idea. For relativity, it is Einstein's $E = mc^2$. For quantum mechanics, it is Planck's $E = hv$.

De Broglie reasoned that if $E = mc^2$ and $E = hv$, then it must be the case that $mc^2 = hv$. This says that mass equals frequency. In other words, mass is the same thing as frequency. Strangely, mass and frequency are properties of completely different kinds of things. Mass is a property of objects. Frequency, on the other hand, is a property of waves. To say that mass is the same thing as frequency is to say that particles are the same thing as waves. He had uncovered wave/particle duality.

To equate particles and waves seems to commit what philosophers call a category mistake. A category mistake is exactly what it sounds like: putting something in the wrong category. Particles are objects. They are self-contained entities. They have a location in space. Waves are not independent things. A medium is required to have a wave.

Particles and waves are not only different things; they are different types of things. To equate them the way de Broglie did is to make a category mistake—unless quantum mechanics comes in.

The Light Problem

In discovering that white light was composed of all the other colors, Isaac Newton posited the corpuscular theory of light according to which light is made of particles. His corpuscular theory was eventually replaced with the new wave theory: Light is a wave. Then, quantum theory started. The first theoretical uses of the quantum were Planck with blackbody radiation and Einstein with the photoelectric effect.

In both cases, light was treated as a particle when it was emitted or absorbed, but both of them still treated it as a wave when it traveled or interacted with matter or other light. This raises the question of whether light is a wave or a particle. De Broglie says that maybe it is both, but it can't be both.

The state equation for quantum mechanics is the Schrödinger equation. When we solve the equation in a particular context for a particular observable quantity, the result is not a single value for the quantity. It is a combination of every possible outcome coupled with a measure of the probability that the system will be found to have that value.

The problem is that we never see systems in this superposed state of all of its possible states. The law of nature tells us what nature looks like when we are not looking, but when we measure it, it changes. This is the so-called measurement problem.

The Double-Slit Experiment

The problem is best illustrated with the famous double-slit experiment. This experiment was first carried out by Thomas Young in the late 1800s. Light from a coherent source is sent through two small slits. When the light hits a screen in front of the slits, there will be a series of bright and dark stripes. This is explained by considering light to be a wave.

The color of the light is a function of the length of the wave, and the brightness is a function of the height of the wave. Because the two slits act as light sources for waves that are synchronized, in the middle, the two waves will add. This means that the light will be twice as bright.

Moving slightly to the side will cause one wave to take a little less time to get there and the other a little more time to get there. This means that the waves are out of phase. Moving a precise amount to the side will cause the waves to become completely out of sync. The top of one wave will hit at the trough of the other. As a result, the waves will cancel each other out, and there will be a dark spot. Moving more will result in alternating dark and bright spots. This result was used by Young to hold light to be a wave.

Photons and the Double-Slit Experiment

From Planck and Einstein, we know that light is quantized. It comes in packets that cannot be divided. We call these photons. Consider Young's experiment again, but this time, imagine that it involves sending only one photon at a time. Because it is the smallest unit of light and we are only sending one, then it will have a choice. It could go through the left slit or the right slit. Then, there should be a single flash somewhere on the screen where the photon hits after going through the slit of its choice.

That is not what happens. We see the striped pattern on the other side. This means that there was the adding and subtracting of waves going through both slits. In turn, the photon theory is wrong. Light is a wave, and it appears we need to throw away the quantum theory.

However, consider one more addition to the experiment: a photodetector that will tell us which slit the photon goes through. The detector tells us that the photon went through one and only one slit. On the screen, we see single flashes of light randomly distributed. There used to be dark spots, but now there are flashes exactly there from time to time.

Imagine that the detectors are no longer operative. Now, the light/dark bands reappear. If we look to see which slit the light goes through, it acts like a particle and only goes through one slit. If we don't look, it acts like a wave and goes through both and adds and subtracts with itself. It knows what we are looking for and acts accordingly.

This is the measurement problem in action. When we do not have the photodetectors in place, then there is no measurement of the photon, and it is in its superposed state of going through both the left and the right slit. That is what gives us the light and dark bands. But when we do have the photodetectors in place, we are making a measurement, and the superposition reduces to just one of the values: left or right. The result is a randomly placed flash on the screen.

When the test is designed for waves, light is a wave. When it is designed for particles, light is a particle. The same thing happens when this experiment uses electrons, complete atoms, and molecules.

Abandoning Realism

Gustav Bergmann was a philosopher, mathematician, and physicist who worked briefly with Albert Einstein. In his article "The Logic of Quanta," Bergmann takes quantum mechanics to be a quintessentially empiricist theory. The theory, he argues, is a collection of rules governing measurements. Measurements are the result of observations, and theories tell us about those measurements.

Are light and subatomic constituents really waves or particles? This is not the sort of question science deals with. Is there a measurement problem in quantum mechanics? It is only a problem for realists.

The Schrödinger equation, when solved, provides a superposed set of possibilities, with each possibility multiplied by a coefficient that is a measure of the probability that it will be observed in that state. When we observe the system, we never see the superposition, but only the system with a single property value. It is impossible to predict with absolute certainty which value it will be. This seems to violate causation.

Bergmann is not bothered by any of this. The theory is successful because the Schrödinger equation does give us the correct statistical data about the measurements we will make. Causation is a metaphysical notion that is only required if we are trying to see the invisible forces underneath observable reality. If we are willing to jettison the metaphysics and make science responsible only for correlating our observations, then quantum theory provides us with no concerns.

The problems with the seeming weirdness of quantum mechanics come from the desire to have a realist viewpoint. If we are willing to give up the reality of atoms, then the progress in atomic theory can be seen simply as progress.

For his part, Albert Einstein held that quantum mechanics is incomplete. It is not a finished theory. It is useful as a provisional placeholder but unsuccessful because it does not allow us the realist's picture of the underlying reality.

Some contemporary philosophers have attempted to thread a needle: They hope that accepting quantum mechanics and believing in atoms are not mutually exclusive. One thinker who tries to make this work is Arthur Fine. In his book *The Shaky Game*, he looks at the realism/empiricism debate around quantum theory and tries to forge an intermediary position called the natural ontological attitude, or NOA.

Suggested Reading

Fine, *The Shaky Game*.
Jones, *The Quantum Ten*.
Lovett Cline, *Men Who Made a New Physics*.

QUIZ QUESTIONS

1. De Broglie's equation equates mass with:

   A. Energy.
   B. Temperature.
   C. Color.
   D. Wavelength.

2. True or false: Young provided experimental evidence that light is a particle.

3. Duns Scotus's term *haeccity* translates to:

   A. This-ness.
   B. Invisibility.
   C. Mass.
   D. Presence.

4. Is Bergmann an empiricist or a realist?

ANSWERS KEY CAN BE FOUND ON PAGE 118

WANTED DEAD AND ALIVE: SCHRÖDINGER'S CAT

LECTURE 10

This lecture focuses on the measurement problem by cataloguing the various ways that physicists have proposed solving it. The problem calls for an odd type of solution: an interpretation. The word *interpretation* here has the same meaning as it does when used in logic. For example, consider this sentence, which has two made-up terms: "There is a wiw on the xax." The truth of that sentence depends on the interpretation of the meaning of the terms *wiw* and *xax*.

A Confusing Cat

A prominent example of strangeness is Schrödinger's equation. When we solve Schrödinger's equation, we get a mathematical combination of every possible state a system could be in. This combination is the state of superposition. The problem is that we never see things in their superposed state. Every measurement we make yields a single value. This is a law of nature that describes nature as it is never observed.

A cat can be used to illustrate this problem. Imagine a cat in a cage covered by a box. We cannot see inside. Outside the box is a button. When we push the button, two electrons are emitted, which are spin-correlated. Spin is a physical quantity and has only two values: up and down. To satisfy conservation laws, when one of the particles is up, the other is down. According to quantum mechanics, before we measure the spin, the two particles are both in superposed states.

Inside the box, a spin detector is set up so that the spin of one of the electrons is measured. The spin detector is connected to a circuit, which is connected to a canister of poison. If the detected spin is up, then nothing happens. If the detected spin is down, then the circuit causes the container to be opened, the poison released, and the cat killed.

Before we look inside the box, the cat is in a state of superposition of alive and dead. This is a strange metaphysical combination we have never observed in reality and cannot make sense of. The interpretations of quantum mechanics are attempts to fill in the story to make that make sense.

> Some of the treatments of interpretations in this lecture follow discussions in David Z. Albert's book *Quantum Mechanics and Experience*. Albert works out exactly what is meant by certain interpretations. In particular, this lecture focuses on Einstein's statistical ensemble view, the Copenhagen interpretation, the collapse interpretations, and the many-worlds interpretation.

DAVID Z. ALBERT

Einstein's Concerns

For Einstein, it was a matter of metaphysical commitment that the world was causally deterministic. Einstein believed that the universe was a well-ordered system that ran according to absolute laws, which the human mind was capable of discovering.

Quantum mechanics is not wrong, he argues, but the lack of cause and effect in the measurement problem means that the theory only tells us part of the story. The theory is incomplete. We should think of it like we think of statistical mechanics. If we want to talk about the behavior of a gas, it is too complicated to model mathematically. We can, however, come up with statistical models and speak in terms of ensembles of microstates corresponding to measurable macrostates. We use probabilities to describe what is happening to the collection of molecules.

The same thing applies, Einstein argues, with respect to quantum mechanics. There must be a way to determine what is happening at the micro level that would allow us to know exactly through cause and effect what the values of the measured properties are.

Einstein's account has the virtue of doing away with the strangeness of Heisenberg's uncertainty relation and the measurement problem. The cat is alive or dead. The probabilities are the result of our lack of knowledge about reality, not in reality itself.

While it possesses this virtue, it also possesses the vice of being provably wrong. This was shown by the physicist John Bell. It turns out that quantum mechanics gets it right. There are no hidden variables. The strangeness is here to stay; we just have to figure out some way to make sense of it. We need an interpretation.

The Copenhagen Interpretation

The most straightforward interpretation came from Niels Bohr, Werner Heisenberg, and the rest of the group at the Bohr Institute in Copenhagen. This is the Copenhagen interpretation. According to the Copenhagen interpretation, particles don't have values until they are measured.

The theory works. It gives an account of the quantum world that gets every prediction correct. That is all a theory is supposed to do, but the Copenhagen interpretation is unsatisfying to many.

The Collapse Interpretation

John von Neumann advocated the collapse interpretation. This holds that the superposed state is descriptive of reality. Reality is in the combination of all possible states until the observation is made.

At the instant the observation is made, something happens, and this superposition of every possible state instantaneously and randomly collapses into one of the possible states. Observation is interference with the system. To measure a system is to operate on it. This has the effect of changing the system.

A more substantive extension of the interpretation was given by Eugene Wigner. The question we have to ask for this extension is what part of the interaction causes the collapse.

There seem to be three phases to an observation. First, the measuring instrument interacts with the system to be measured. Second, the system inside the measuring instrument is changed to be able to report the measurement. Finally, someone looks at the scale, the screen, or the printout and interprets the reading.

Wigner asks: Of these three phases, which one is different? The first one is just matter interacting with matter. The second one is a resulting material change within a material system. The third state is unusual. It is matter interacting with mind. The last phase requires intelligence making sense of the measurement.

Because the third step is a completely different kind of thing, maybe it is the cause of the collapse. The superposition collapses because the material world is interacting with the mental world.

The Many-Worlds Interpretation

The many-worlds interpretation comes from Hugh Everett III. In the late 1950s, he decided that perhaps instead of having to explain how the laws were violated, causing the collapse of the wave function, that we simply embrace the theory and the wave function.

Everett argues that when we perform an observation, what happens is not that the wave function in this world collapses. Instead, this world splits into multiple worlds, each one claiming one of the values of the property state being measured.

Going back to the example of the cat: When we open the box to see what state the cat is in—dead or alive—we are seeing for this world. However, no matter which world we happen to occupy, there is another world just like this one where we find Fluffy in the other state.

Suggested Reading

Albert, *Quantum Mechanics and Experience.*
Bohm, *Wholeness and the Implicate Order.*

QUIZ QUESTIONS

1. True or false: We observe matter in a superposed state.

2. Match the physicist to the interpretation of quantum mechanics:

    A. Einstein.   i. Pilot wave.
    B. Von Neumann.   ii. Many-worlds.
    C. Everett.   iii. Copenhagen.
    D. De Broglie.   iv. Hidden variables.
    E. Bohr.   v. Collapse.

3. What collapses in the collapse interpretation?

    A. Space.
    B. Superposition.
    C. Duality.
    D. Properties.

4. True or false: Einstein demanded that all laws of nature be deterministic.

ANSWERS KEY CAN BE FOUND ON PAGE 118

THE DREAM OF GRAND UNIFICATION

LECTURE 11

With respect to scientific theories, this lecture is interested in the following epistemological question: What gives us grounds to believe that a given scientific theory is true? In other words, what are the marks of a successful scientific theory?

William Whewell

One relevant reasonable virtue was proposed by the 19th-century scientist and philosopher William Whewell. He noted the most successful theories in the history of science shared a common property, unifying our picture of the universe. Successful theories were not only able to account for the phenomena they were designed to explain but could also be used to explain other areas of study.

The term he created for this property of unexpected expansion of the realm of explanation is *consilience*. A theory is consilient if it is able to account for what had previously been considered disparate areas of science.

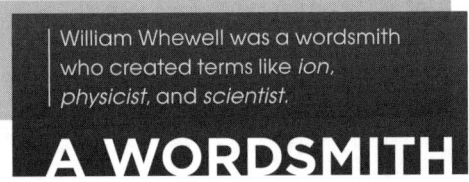

William Whewell was a wordsmith who created terms like *ion*, *physicist*, and *scientist*.

A WORDSMITH

Karl Popper

A second, seemingly similar virtue for acceptable theories was provided by the 20th-century philosopher Karl Popper. Popper contended that better theories are bolder theories. We ought to reward theories that are the riskiest, the most general, and the broadest in scope.

Popper also remarked on the property of falsifiability. A proposition or a theory is only scientific if it is falsifiable. A sentence is false if what it says about the world is not how the world is. A sentence is falsified if it is shown to be false. A sentence or theory is falsifiable if and only if there are potential falsifiers. It does not mean the sentence is false. Rather, it means that it could be if the world were a certain way. Maximal falsifiability is maximal riskiness, and that is what we should celebrate in science.

Progress

James Clerk Maxwell brought together bits and pieces of work on electricity and magnetism into a single coherent theory of electromagnetism. This resulted in an account of optics, the physics of light. Einstein's theory of special relativity brought together mechanics with Maxwell's electrodynamics. His theory of general relativity then also included gravitation. Both steps showed consilience with an increase in falsifiability.

The process of physics up through the middle of the 20th century was a story of increasing unification. Then came quantum mechanics. In the middle of the 20th century, physics had two theories: general relativity and quantum mechanics. Both were tremendously falsifiable but had not been falsified.

Each made slews of correct predictions about the world. The challenge was to bring them together into a single picture of the universe, which would solve the whole problem of the universe.

A Difficult Task

In 1935, Albert Einstein along with Boris Pedolsky and Nathan Rosen proposed a thought experiment that illustrated the trouble that would keep quantum mechanics and general relativity from being easily assimilated. Electrons have a property called spin. Mathematically, it behaves like rotation. It is possible to create pairs of electrons that are spin-correlated—that is, in order to obey a conservation law, the electrons will have opposite spins. If electron A has something called spin up, then electron B will have spin down, or vice versa.

However, an important detail from quantum mechanics is that when we do not observe a system, it will be in a state of superposition. It will be in a combination of every possible state it could be in. The Schrödinger equation gives us a mathematical combination that describes how things are, and this holds until a measurement is taken.

LECTURE 11 ◂ The Dream of Grand Unification

If we create these spin-correlated electrons but don't look at either one, both are in the superposed state of up and down. The instant we look at one, it will go from the superposed state into a single value of the property. Because the two electrons are spin-correlated, if we observe electron 1 and find it to be spin up, electron 2 must acquire the spin value down.

Now suppose we created the particles at a facility at the University of Kansas in the middle of the United States and then sent the electrons east and west—one to Columbia University in New York and the other to Stanford in California—but measured neither. Electron A is on the East Coast in a superposed state and electron B on the West Coast in a superposed state.

Imagine that someone becomes impatient and checks the spin of the East Coast electron. Because the measurement was taken, electron 1 acquires a single spin value. For this example, that value is up. This means that at that very instant, electron 2 in California had to go from a state of superposition to the state of spin down.

The question is: How did electron 2 know that electron 1 was measured? The only way it could know is if a signal was sent. To get across the width of the United States, that signal would take time. Making that time gap small enough forces the signal from electron 1 to electron 2 to move faster than the speed of light. However, according to the theory of relativity, no signal can move faster than the speed of light. Quantum mechanics says that it would have to in cases like this. Physicists refer to this as spooky action at a distance. It is ruled out by relativity but required by quantum mechanics. The two theories seem to be incompatible.

A New Theory

Einstein believed it would be necessary to replace quantum mechanics with a better theory. The better theory came, but it did not replace quantum mechanics. Rather, it extended it.

There are four seemingly distinct forces in the universe known to us. The two we have known about the longest are gravity and electromagnetism. To explain how electricity and magnetism work, Maxwell and his teacher Michael Faraday developed the notion of a field. A field is a space with a small arrow attached to each point of the space. The arrows at each point will change their size and direction, but they do so in concert with the arrows at the points around them so that changes are smooth.

Einstein used this idea as well when accounting for gravitation. The theory of gravitation is about the behavior of the gravitational field. It seemed to many, including Einstein, that it should be possible to take these two field theories and bring them together into a theory about one field that accounts for both the electromagnetic and gravitational forces. This would be a unified field theory. The project would occupy Einstein until his death.

Theodor Kaluza and Oskar Klein independently worked on such a theory. Their Kaluza-Klein model showed great promise for a time. For technical reasons, the theory did not work, but it presented the idea of adding extra dimensions and rolling them up at points.

Progress Continues

This project of finding a unified field theory for the two original forces of gravity and electromagnetism was eclipsed by the progress of physics when researchers started looking more deeply at atoms. J. J. Thomson discovered the electron. Atoms were not the uncuttable bits that the classical Greeks considered, but rather they had parts, one of which was negatively charged. He embedded these negatively charged nuggets in a goo of positivity in his plum pudding model of the atom.

That model was rejected when Ernest Rutherford discovered the nucleus. The positivity was jammed into a tiny, hard kernel. This gave us the solar system model of the universe, with the nucleus playing the part of the sun and the electrons revolving around as planets.

There are three problems with this model. First, if the nucleus was made up of positively charged protons jammed together very tightly, the electromagnetic charge would blow them up. Positive and positive forces repel, and they repel harder the closer they are. There would be no way the nucleus could hold together.

The second problem for the solar system model of the atom is radioactivity. Every once in a while, at predictable rates, a particle will shoot out of the nucleus with high energy. This was a force called weak nuclear force. This joined three other forces: gravity, the strong nuclear force that hold things together, and the electromagnetic force. The electromagnetic force can be repulsive, but it is overmatched by the strong nuclear force.

The third problem for the solar system model was this: Moving electrical charges create a magnetic field, and this requires energy. If the electrons are going around the nucleus, they would be losing energy and thereby spiraling into the nucleus. Atoms should be collapsing. They should not be stable, but they are.

Unifications

The answer to this came from Niels Bohr, and that answer launched quantum mechanics. The emergence of the two new forces were entangled through the investigation of the atom with quantum theory. The result of this is that when electromagnetism was brought into unification, it was not, as Einstein hoped, a unified field theory of electromagnetism and gravity that emerged. Rather, it was a unification of the new nuclear forces and electromagnetism in the advanced quantum theories.

The first unification was the electromagnetic force with the weak nuclear force. This gave us quantum electrodynamics. Next, the strong force was unified with the others, showing that three of the four different forces we observe in nature are just different aspects of a single force. This gave us quantum field theory.

These were unifications that would have pleased both Whewell and Popper. Each step achieved the sort of conceptual coherence that Whewell described with his notion of consilience, and doing so predicted the existence of new particles and new phenomena that could be observed. Quantum field theory was bold and made risky predictions that required empirical data. Popper, like Whewell, would approve.

This left us with two distinct field theories. General relativity gives a description of the gravitational field. Quantum field theory gives us a description of the field that accounts for the other three forces: electromagnetism and the weak and strong nuclear forces. That is where matters have stood for decades. Both field theories are right about everything they predict, but they are seemingly incompatible. They can't both be right, but neither is wrong.

The Standard Model

Quantum field theory has been used to develop the Standard Model, which categorizes every particle and force in the universe. Even the four forces can be thought of as particles that are exchanged when a system experiences an interaction involving that force.

The Standard Model divides things in the universe into two large categories according to the sort of mathematical statistics that govern their behavior. Those that are governed by Fermi-Dirac statistics are called fermions. Those that obey Bose-Einstein statistics are called bosons and are what we usually think of as forces.

Fermions come in two types. One type is the set of quarks. These come in three pairs—up, down; top, bottom; and strange, charmed. These make up the protons and neutrons. The other flavor is the set of leptons. These also come in three pairs: electron and electron neutrino, muon and muon neutrino, and tau and tau neutrino. Bosons also come in two flavors. Gauge bosons are the virtual particles related to the four forces, and the lone scalar boson is the Higgs boson, which is responsible for giving particles their mass.

String Theory

First proposed in the 1980s, string theory provides us with a possible picture of what is giving rise to the Standard Model. Imagine a field with something attached to each point of the field: a string. Strings can be open, stretch out like a line, and vibrate in a number of ways. They can also be closed—that is, a loop that also can vibrate in a number of ways.

The modes of the open vibrations are correlated with the different fermions. The different modes of closed-loop vibrations are correlated with the different bosons. String theory has the great virtue of giving us an image that explains everything in the Standard Model. It also appears to have the greater virtue of being able to do it in a way that accounts for the general theory of relativity. If we take the universe to be the way string theorists claim, then we may be well on the path to a complete unified field theory of everything.

This, its supporters argue, demonstrates its likely truth. Unification is a sign of truth, and string theory is the ultimate unifier. Therefore, string theory is probably the ultimate truth. However, there are opponents of the theory. They point out that while it is true that we have consilience with string theory, it lacks falsifiability.

Suggested Reading

Greene, *The Elegant Universe*.
Smolin, Lee. *The Trouble with Physics*.
Woit, Peter. *Not Even Wrong*.

QUIZ QUESTIONS

1. Who coined the terms *scientist*, *physicist*, *linguistics*, and *ion*?

2. True or false: For Popper, all falsifiable sentences are false.

3. The spooky action-at-a-distance required by quantum mechanics in the EPR paradox violates what other theory?

4. The particles that carry forces in the Standard Model are called:

    A. Bosons.
    B. Fermions.
    C. Electrons.
    D. Quarks.

5. Which epistemological virtue do opponents of string theory argue that the theory lacks: Whewell's consilience or Popper's falsificationism?

ANSWERS KEY CAN BE FOUND ON PAGE 118

THE PHYSICS OF GOD

LECTURE 12

Perhaps the metaphysical question that has garnered the most interest in intellectual history concerns the existence of God. Arguments for and against the existence of a creator come in several types. The laws of physics have been used on both sides of the debate.

Early Thinking

In the 1700s, some figures, like Baron d'Holbach, contended that the system of the universe Isaac Newton gave us leads directly to the lack of a need for any sort of divinity at all. In his masterwork *The System of Nature*, d'Holbach dismisses philosophers who thought that God was necessary to explain the continual motion of the heavens.

The opposite line was taken by many philosophers, such as William Paley. In his book *Natural Theology*, Paley contends that the complexity of the working of the universe is a mark of its design. Advocating the teleological argument for the existence of God, or the argument from design, Paley argues that the world shows interrelated structures, and those entail intelligent creation.

For instance, the structured complexity of a watch requires a watchmaker—that is, an intelligent designer who crafted the intricate working system. Paley points to aspects of living beings and argues that the structure is more complex than any watch. If there is an inference of intelligent design in the case of the timepiece, there must be also in the case of living beings.

This biological argument became less influential after the work of Charles Darwin. Evolutionary theory gave a purely materialistic account for the properties of different species. Paley's argument turns on the complex elements of the anatomy of animals. That complexity could be seen after Darwin as the result of purely material circumstances. By the end of the 19th century, the teleological argument for the existence of God fell out of favor.

The Argument Reemerges

Late-20th-century physics brought the argument back to life. The Standard Model is our best account of the laws governing everything except gravitation. The general theory of relativity accounts for that. All of these equations have constants within them—that is, terms that have to be included in the equations to make the units come out right.

Physicist Robert Dicke pointed out in his article "Dirac's Cosmology and Mach's Principle" that we can arithmetically combine these constants to give rise to dimensionless numbers—that is, we can multiply and divide these constants in combinations that make all the units cancel out. Numbers that should have nothing to do with each other—things like the age of the universe, the mass of the proton, and the gravitational constant—seem to be intricately related when properly multiplied and divided by each other. That is strange.

Physicist Martin Rees has argued that it seems to be the result of the fine-tuning of the universe. If these constants were slightly different in numerical value, the result would be a universe completely incapable of giving rise to life. Richard Swinburn, a professor, contends that the facts arising from contemporary physics show an interrelation and a sensitivity that cannot but resurrect the teleological argument: The intricacy of the universe implies the existence of an intelligent creator God.

Denying Fine-Tuning: Necessity

A second approach to the question of fine-tuning is to deny the notion of tuning at all. This approach takes two very different forms. These are the necessity and contingency approaches to denying design.

The necessity approach to denying design looks at the history of physics and sees a process. That process is one of unification, which started with a vast array of widely different sorts of phenomena and boiled it down to a small handful of laws and entities.

The history has led to the current state, which has given us the Standard Model, a rather minimalist accounting of the basic components of the universe. We have laws that, while not in their finished state, account for most of what we see. Those laws have a certain form. All include a few constants, which need empirical determination at this time in the process.

As the process works on, these constants may turn out to be interdependent, thereby decreasing their number. Indeed, the number may even decrease to zero. The ultimate form of the laws of nature may themselves decrease to a single principle containing no underdetermined quantities. If this is the case, then the fine-tuning question goes away. The whole question was a result of our lack of knowledge of the actual laws of nature.

Denying Fine-Tuning: Contingency

The contingency approach to denying design takes a different line, arguing that there is not actually anything here that needs explaining. It contends that things just are the way they are. If that is the case, there is nothing to explain.

Elliot Sober weighs in on this question of fine-tuning arguments in philosophy of physics. His argument does not make the move of the necessity approach. We don't need to assume anything about the ultimate form of the laws of nature. We can take them as they are. We can also grant that the universal laws could be of a different form and that the constants could be of a different value. We will allow all of this to be contingent—that is, not necessary.

If all of this could have been otherwise, but turned out to be as it is, then it seems we need an explanation. However, Sober argues that is not the case. Just because something highly improbable occurs does not mean that it was designed. Improbable things accidentally happen all the time. The key is to look at them from the proper direction.

For instance, imagine a lottery: If the lottery sells 250,000 tickets, the odds of winning are very tiny. As such, it is more than unlikely that any given person will win. However, it is certain that someone will win.

Sober argues that the fine-tuning argument makes the mistake of looking from the wrong direction. We are holding the winning lottery ticket. We are in a universe that supports life.

Inflation

At one point, cosmologists were puzzled by strange phenomena. The universe seemed geometrically flat and thermally harmonious in a way that should not be the case if far-flung parts of the cosmos cannot communicate with each other.

The answer to both of these questions came from cosmologist Alan Guth, who proposed the idea of inflation. According to this account, not long after the big bang, the young universe underwent a short period of incredibly rapid expansion. Because the universe had been small before the expansion, the parts were close enough to be in communication, so equilibrium could be established. It would then be maintained after the expansion. The expansion would smooth out the geometry because everything became rapidly stretched.

Before the inflation, when the universe was young, small, and hot, the forces of the universe may have been undifferentiated. There may have only been one force. But as the universe cooled, the different forces separated out from each other. Physicists call this symmetry breaking.

The way the symmetry breaks may be a function of accidental properties. It might not be a necessary result. This might mean that it was the uncertainty around the instant of inflation of our universe that set the laws in their particular form and the constants at their particular values for our universe.

This has given rise to the idea that perhaps this inflation occurs multiple times. Maybe ours is just one universe that started with a big bang and then inflated like a bubble. Perhaps there are others.

Philosophers like John Leslie, an emeritus professor from the University of Guelph, see this as a naturalistic alternative to the theological argument from design based on the fine-tuning of the universe. If reality gives itself multiple tries at forming universes, then what we see is a form of natural selection that is not unlike what we see in Darwin's biological form.

If there are multiple bubble universes, each undergoing inflation under slightly different initial conditions, then there will be multiple universes with multiple laws and constant values. Most will fail to develop because the laws and constants don't allow matter to form or, if so, stars burn too quickly or slowly to allow for the development.

However, buying enough cosmic lottery tickets eventually produces a winner. Enough tickets will be picked that a universe with the proper characteristics will accidentally be brought into being. Life may happen to be created in it. This life may morph and mutate until it becomes sentient and intelligent. Ultimately, perhaps, this life will understand the working of the universe that gave rise to it.

Suggested Reading

Davies, *Cosmic Jackpot*.
Leslie, *Modern Cosmology and Philosophy*.

QUIZ QUESTIONS

1. Who proposed the mechanical philosophy?

   A. Aristotle.
   B. Descartes.
   C. Newton.
   D. Einstein.

2. Which view posits a God that is ever present within creation: deism or theism?

3. True or false: Baron d'Holbach was an atheist.

4. What is tuned in the fine-tuning argument?

   A. The collapse of the wave function.
   B. Mental thoughts and the physical world.
   C. The structure of the equations of the laws of nature.
   D. The constants in the laws of nature.

5. What do the bubbles in the so-called cosmic bubble bath represent?

ANSWERS KEY CAN BE FOUND ON PAGE 118

QUIZ ANSWER KEY

Lecture 1

1. C.
2. Astronomy is the study of the universe. Cosmology is the study of the origin of the universe.
3. "Before experience."
4. Epistemology.
5. How to tell if a sentence has meaning.

Lecture 2

1. A.
2. True.
3. We start by observing the world around us, but as science progresses, we adopt an increasingly abstract perspective.
4. True.
5. David Hilbert.

Lecture 3

1. B.
2. False.
3. Cause.
4. The word *nomological* means "related to laws."

Lecture 4

1. Newton is a substantivalist. Leibniz is a relationist.
2. D.
3. General.
4. False.
5. A.

Lecture 5

1. Relative.
2. True.
3. D.
4. A-time.
5. True.

Lecture 6

1. E.
2. False.
3. Edwin Hubble.
4. Big Bang.
5. B.

QUIZ ANSWER KEY

Lecture 7
1. D.
2. True.
3. Phlogiston.
4. A.
5. False.

Lecture 8
1. False.
2. Chemistry.
3. Niels Bohr.
4. Erwin Schrödinger.
5. Two and three, respectively.

Lecture 9
1. D.
2. False.
3. A.
4. An empiricist.

Lecture 10
1. False.
2. A = iv, B = v, C = ii, D = i, E = iii.
3. B.
4. True.

Lecture 11
1. William Whewell.
2. False.
3. Special relativity.
4. A.
5. Falsificationism.

Lecture 12
1. B.
2. Theism.
3. True.
4. D.
5. Individual universes.

BIBLIOGRAPHY

Achinstein, Peter. *Speculation Within and About Science*. New York: Oxford, 2019. A contemporary philosophical discussion of the roles of speculation and simplicity in the scientific method.

Albert, David Z. *Quantum Mechanics and Experience*. Cambridge: Harvard University Press, 1992. A treatment of the theory of quantum mechanics and in-depth analysis of the proposed interpretations of the theory.

Alexander, H. G. *The Leibniz/Clarke Correspondence*. The letters back and forth between Gottfried Leibniz and Isaac Newton's defender Samuel Clarke concerning the nature of space and God.

Aquinas, Thomas. *Summa Theologiae*. Lander: Aquinas Institute, 2012. A major historical work of philosophy and theology that sets out Saint Thomas's proofs for the existence of God and other major views on the nature of knowledge and reality.

Aristotle. *Physics*. Lincoln: University of Nebraska Press, 1961. A masterwork by the great Greek thinker that sets out both his system of the universe and his understanding of the nature of science and cause.

Ayer, A. J. *Language, Truth, and Logic*. New York: Dover, 1952. A discussion of the tenants and central problems addressed by logical positivism.

———. *Logical Positivism*. New York: Free Press, 1959. An edited volume that includes the seminal articles written by the logical positivists, arranged by topic.

Bell, J. S. *Speakable and Unspeakable in Quantum Mechanics*. New York: Cambridge, 1987. A collection of papers about the nature and meaning of quantum mechanics by the physicist who gave us the Bell inequalities showing Einstein's favored approach to be untenable.

Bergmann, Gustav. "The Logic of Quanta" *American Journal of Physics* 15, no. 5: 397–497. A member of the school of logical positivism arguing that the seeming problems of quantum mechanics vanish if we think of it only as a theory of measurement, not as a description of the world.

Bergmann, Peter. *The Riddle of Gravitation*. New York: Dover, 1968. A good discussion of the history of cosmology from one of Einstein's assistants.

Blackburn, Simon. *Think: A Compelling Introduction to Philosophy*. New York: Oxford University Press, 1999. An accessible and fun introduction to the various fields and questions in philosophy.

Bohm, David. *Wholeness and the Implicate Order*. New York: Ark, 1980. A popular book by one of the physicists who championed a holistic understanding of the universe based on his work in quantum mechanics.

Boslough, John. *Masters of Time: Cosmology at the End of Innocence*. Reading: Addison-Wesley, 1992. A well-written popular account of the development of cosmology through the middle and end of the 20th century.

Carnap, Rudolf. *The Logical Structure of the World: Pseudo-Problems in Philosophy*. Berkeley: University of California Press, 1967. Seminal work in logical positivism by the figure most strongly associated with the movement.

Cartwright, Nancy. *How the Laws of Physics Lie*. New York: Oxford University Press, 1983. A provocative argument that separates scientific truth from explanatory power, arguing that our best scientific explanations are literally false and should be.

Davies, Paul. *Cosmic Jackpot: Why Our Universe Is Just Right for Life*. Boston: Houghton-Mifflin, 2007. A survey of the range of views accounting for the fine-tuning argument.

Descartes, René. *Discourse on Method, Optics, Geometry, and Meteorology*. Indianapolis: Bobbs-Merrill, 1965. The work where Descartes not only writes "I think, therefore I am" but sets out his vision of philosophy as the foundation of the sciences and works out the basis of what would become analytic geometry.

Earman, John. *World Enough and Space-Time: Absolute versus Relational Theories of Space and Time*. Cambridge: MIT Press, 1989. A masterwork by one of the biggest names in contemporary philosophy of physics examining the historical development of the argument concerning the reality of space.

Einstein, Albert. *Relativity: The Special and General Theory—A Clear Explanation that Anyone Can Understand*. New York: Wings, 1961. Einstein's own popular explanation of the theory of relativity.

———. *Sidelights on Relativity*. New York: Dover, 1922. A small collection of essays about relativity theory from Einstein himself.

Einstein, Albert, et al. *The Principle of Relativity*. New York: Dover, 1952. A collection of the original scientific papers central to the discovery and development of the theory of relativity through its first couple of decades.

Ferris, Timothy. *Coming of Age in the Milky Way*. New York: Anchor, 1988. One of the classic popular treatments of the history of cosmology.

Feynman, Richard. *The Character of Physical Law*. Cambridge: MIT Press, 1964. A reflection on the foundational concepts of physics by the noted Nobel laureate.

Field, Hartry. *Science without Numbers: A Defense of Nominalism*. Princeton: Princeton University Press, 1980. A technically difficult book that seeks to reconstruct the foundations of physics using concepts but no numbers.

Fine, Arthur. *The Shaky Game: Einstein, Realism, and the Quantum Theory*. Chicago: University of Chicago Press, 1996. A technical work in philosophy examining in detail Einstein's concerns with quantum mechanics and evaluating the arguments in a way that tries to find a middle ground between Einstein and his opponents developing the Copenhagen interpretation of quantum mechanics.

Friedman, Michael. *Foundations of Space-Time Theories: Relativistic Physics and Philosophy of Science*. Princeton: Princeton University Press, 1983. One of the great works of contemporary philosophy of physics in which various space-time theories are worked out formally in order to demonstrate the full set of metaphysical assumptions underlying them.

Glymour, Clark. *Theory and Evidence*. Princeton: Princeton University Press, 1980. A collection of essays from a preeminent contemporary philosopher of physics examining the nature of scientific evidence and concepts in physics.

Greene, Brian. *The Elegant Universe: Superstrings, Hidden Dimensions, and the Quest for an Ultimate Theory*. New York: Vintage Books, 1999. A popular account of string theory written by one of the physicists at the center of its development.

Grunbaum, Adolf. "The Pseudo-Problem of Creation in Physical Cosmology." 1989. *Philosophy of Science* 56, no. 3: 373–394.

Hempel, Carl G. *Aspects of Scientific Explanation.* New York: Free Press, 1965. A book of essays concerning the scientific method, including the seminal essay "Studies in the Logical of Scientific Explanation."

Holbach, Paul Henri Thiry (Baron d'Holbach). *The System of Nature: Laws of the Moral and Physical World.* An Enlightenment masterpiece that argues that human reason is sufficient for the understanding of everything.

Horwich, Paul. *Asymmetries in Time: Problems in the Philosophy of Science.* A technical work by a prominent philosopher of physics examining the physical and philosophical problems concerning the nature and direction of time.

Huggett, Nick. *Space from Zeno to Einstein: Classic Readings with a Contemporary Commentary.* Cambridge: MIT Press, 1999. An edited collection of the most important writings by physicists and philosophers from antiquity to the 20th century on the nature of space.

Jones, Sheilla. *The Quantum Ten.* New York: Oxford, 2008. A history of the development of quantum mechanics through the first half of the 20th century.

Leslie, John. *Modern Cosmology and Philosophy.* New York: Prometheus Books, 1998. An edited volume containing a wide variety of voices and viewpoints on the philosophical questions raised by issues in cosmology.

Lewis, David. "Paradoxes of Time Travel." *Philosophical Quarterly* 13, no. 2: 145–152. An attempt to dissolve the logical problems associated with traveling back in time and acting in a way that would affect the future.

Lovett Cline, Barbara. *Men Who Made a New Physics*. A wonderfully written popular account of the development of quantum mechanics from Rutherford to Bohr and Einstein.

Mach, Ernst. *The Science of Mechanics: A Critical and Historical Account of its Development.* Evanston: Open Court, 1960. The classic text setting out the view of positivism wherein the only things we should accept as real are those things that can be observed.

McTaggart, J. M. E. "The Unreality of Time." *Mind* vol. 17. A classic article that distinguishes between two pictures of time and argues that they both apply, making time a self-contradictory notion and therefore unreal.

Newton, Isaac. *Mathematical Principles of Natural Philosophy.* Berkeley: University of California Press, 1934. The masterwork of one of history's greatest geniuses that sets out the theories of mechanics and gravitation that would be the heart of physics for 300 years.

Perrin, Jean. *Atoms*. Woodbridge: Oxbow Press, 1990. A discussion by the Nobel laureate who established once and for all that atoms exist on how he did it.

Poincaré, Henri. *Science and Hypothesis.* New York: Dover, 1952. A popular philosophical book by one of the great minds in mathematics and physics considering the foundational concepts underlying all of physics.

Popper, Karl. *The Logic of Scientific Discovery.* New York: Basic, 1959. A classic work in the philosophy of science according to which a proposition is scientific if and only if there are possible observation sentences that, if true, would render the sentence false.

Price, Huw. *Time's Arrow and Archimedes' Point*. New York: Oxford, 1997. A technical philosophical work that challenges the reigning orthodoxy about the nature of time.

Pullman, Bernard. *The Atom in the History of Human Thought*. New York: Oxford, 1998. A popular account of the development of the notion of atoms and the development of atomic theory from antiquity to the 20th century.

Putnam, Hilary. *Mathematics, Matter, and Method: Philosophical Papers* vol. 1. New York: Cambridge University Press, 1975. A collection of Putnam's most important works in philosophy of mathematics and philosophy of science.

Quine, W. V. O. *From a Logical Point of View*. Cambridge: Harvard University Press, 1953. Quine's collection of essays that includes his most famous piece, "Two Dogmas of Empiricism," which undermined logical positivism.

Reichenbach, Hans. *The Philosophy of Space and Time*. New York: Dover, 1958. A founding father of philosophy of physics works out the foundational concepts needed to construct relativistic physics.

———. *The Direction of Time*. Exploration of the ways in which physical theory does and does not select a picture of time that distinguishes between past and future.

Reid, Constance. *Hilbert*. New York: Springer-Verlag, 1970. A fun and accessible biography of one of history's greatest and most entertaining mathematical minds.

Russell, Bertrand. "On the Notion of Cause." *Proceedings of the Aristotelean Society* 13, no. 1: 1–26. The great philosopher's argument that the concept of cause is a needless leftover from previous centuries where explanation required reference to the will of God and therefore should be abandoned in contemporary discourse about science.

Smart, J. J. C. *Philosophy and Scientific Realism.* New York: Humanities, 1963. A book by one of the leading names in philosophy in the mid-20th century defending the view that the elements mentioned in our best scientific theories ought to be considered to be actual parts of the real world.

Smolin, Lee. *The Trouble with Physics: The Rise of String Theory, the Fall of a Science, and What Comes Next.* New York: Houghton-Mifflin, 2006. An account of the rise of string theory from one of the physicists who contributed to it as well as his concerns that the theory has more in terms of public relations than it does in terms of actual scientific support.

Sober, Elliott. "Absence of Evidence and Evidence of Absence: Evidential Transitivity in Connection with Fossils, Fishing, Fine-tuning, and Firing Squads." *Philosophical Studies* vol. 143, 63–90.

Tegmark, Max. "The Mathematical Universe." *Foundations of Physics* 38, no. 2: 101–150. An argument by a leading physical theorist that the reason mathematics works so well in describing the world is that the world is, in fact, mathematical.

Toulmin, Stephen, and Jane Goodfield. *The Fabric of the Heavens: The Development of Astronomy and Dynamics.* New York: Harper & Row, 1965. An accessible discussion of the development of physical theories of motion and astronomy from antiquity through the 20th century.

Van Fraassen, Bas. *The Scientific Image.* New York: Clarendon Press, 1980. A provocative argument from one of the 20th century's most provocative philosophers.

Von Neumann, John. *Logic, Theory of Sets, and Quantum Mechanics*. New York: Pergammon, 1963. A collection of the works of the great mathematical genius including those that considered his work on the logical foundations of quantum mechanics.

Whewell, William. *Theory of the Scientific Method*. Indianapolis: Hackett, 1989. An edited collection of the works of Whewell that focus on the nature of scientific methodology and explanation.

Wigner, Eugene. "The Unreasonable Effectiveness of Mathematics in the Natural Sciences." *Communications on Pure and Applied Mathematics* 13: 1–14. A historically important essay that explores the reasons why mathematics works so well in physics.

Wittgenstein, Ludwig. *Tractatus Logico-Philosophicus*. Atlantic Highlands: Humanities Press, 1922. A seminal work in the history of philosophy that claims to solve or dissolve the problems of philosophy by reducing them to logic.

Woit, Peter. *Not Even Wrong: The Failure of String Theory and the Search for Unity in Physical Law*. New York: Basic Books, 2007. An argument from a leading physicist and critic of string theory setting out the case against it based on the claim that it fails to meet the basic criteria for a theory to be scientific.

Image Credits

3: tiero/iStock/Getty Images Plus; 12: hh5800/iStock/Getty Images Plus; 13: Gerard Edlinck/Gallica Digital Library; 22: Tomwang112/iStock/Getty Images Plus; 23: PanosKarapanagiotis/Getty Images; 31: the-lightwriter/iStock/Getty Images Plus; 33: Kuebi/Wikimedia Commons/Public Domain; 41: Brankospejs/iStock/Getty Images Plus; 42: Philadelphia Museum of Art; 42: Philadelphia Museum of Art; 50: raspirator/iStock/Getty Images Plus; 59: cokada/iStock/Getty Images Plus; 63: Library of Congress, Prints and Photographs Division; 70: agsandrew/iStock/Getty Images Plus; 76: Smithsonian Institution Libraries/flickr/Public Domain; 83: INchendio/iStock/Getty Images Plus; 85: Library of Congress, Prints and Photographs Division; 92: ALexmia/iStock/Getty Images Plus; 95: University of Toronto - Gerstein Science Information Centre/Internet Archive/Public Domain; 99: ArisSu/iStock/Getty Images Plus; 101: LSE Library/flickr/Public Domain; 110: coffeekai/iStock/Getty Images Plus; 111: New York Public Library

NOTES

NOTES